Tortillas, Beans and M-16s

Tortillas, Beans and M-16s
A YEAR WITH THE GUERRILLAS IN EL SALVADOR

Wendy Shaull

PLUTO PRESS
London ● Winchester, Mass

First published 1990 by Pluto Press
345 Archway Road, London N6 5AA
and 8 Winchester Place, Winchester
MA 01890, USA

Copyright © 1990 Wendy Shaull

British Library Cataloguing in Publication Data
Shaull, Wendy
    Tortillas, beans and M-16s : a year with the guerrillas
    in El Salvador.
    1. El Salvador. Political events, 1980-Tricontinental
    Society viewpoints
    I. Title
    972.84'053

ISBN 0–7453–0351–X   hb
ISBN 0–7453–0352–8   pb

Library of Congress Cataloging-in-Publication Data
Shaull, Wendy.
    Tortillas, beans, and M-16s : A year with the guerrillas in El Salvador/
Wendy Shaull.
        p.   cm.
    ISBN 0–7453–0351–X
    ISBN 0–7453–0352–8 (pbk.)
    1. El Salvador–Politics and government–1979-   2. Guerrillas–El
Salvador–History–20th century.   3. Civil-military relations–El
Salvador–History–20th century.   4. Insurgency–El Salvador–
History–20th century.   5. Shaull, Wendy.   I. Title.
F1488.3.S53   1990
972.8405'3–dc20   89–38556
                                                                        CIP

Typeset by Opus, Oxford
Printed in Great Britain by T.J. Press Ltd, Padstow

Contents

Illustrations appear between pages 48 and 49

To Paulo Wright
tortured, killed and disappeared
Brazil 1973

Acknowledgements

To begin with I want to thank my mother and father who have a habit of believing in me and in my projects. I know I'm extremely privileged. Thank you, Mildred and Dick.

My project in El Salvador, of which this book is one of the results, and my second trip down there to retrieve my work, were financed by the International Center for Development Policy in Washington, DC. Thank you Lindsay Mattison.

The freedom to write fulltime, without financial worries, was a gift given by several individuals: my parents, Melinda Rorick and Jack and April Fairweather; and by an institution: the Human Rights Resources Office for Latin America (thank you Chuck Harper), World Council of Churches in Geneva, Switzerland.

Upon sitting down at my typewriter I was unexpectedly presented with another gift: a house to write in on an island off the coast of Rio de Janeiro, Brazil. Thank you Robert and Rosemary Forrester. Thanks for taking care of me and putting up with me for so many months during the weekends.

One last named thank you goes to my publisher Roger van Zwanenberg, who said, 'yes.'

But whether I received financial, residential or spiritual support, each person named and unnamed (and they are many) was saying, 'I believe in what you're doing', which is the greatest gift of all. Thank you then becomes very meager indeed. But I can say no other. Thank you all, very much.

'When history can no longer be written with a pen
it must be written with a gun.'
Agustín Farabundo Martí[1]

Preface

This book is about guerrillas[2] and war in El Salvador.[3] It is a journal of a year lived.

I never intended to write a book – I am, or was, a photojournalist – but we humans are surprising creatures, and my arm was twisted so I gave in.

Many people have asked me why I did such a crazy thing; why I spent a year with the guerrillas in the mountains of El Salvador. At the time it did not seem crazy to me; it seemed a necessity – although not for a year – and there were two reasons for this.

First, in 1983, when I made the decision to carry out this project, there were two wars being fought in Central America that were overtly being financed by my government. One was/is taking place in Nicaragua, the other in El Salvador.

I felt that as a journalist and an American citizen I should know whom my government was fighting against. I think we need to educate ourselves on the wars that our government is abetting or starting. Otherwise, we could suddenly wake up one morning to find ourselves participating in a war that we are, once again, unprepared for and don't understand. A responsible government, in our democratic system, can only be possible when we Americans take the time to learn and to care.

As a photojournalist I had been to Nicaragua several times. Access to the country is, in contrast to El Salvador, very easy. It is a place where many Americans have gone, be it out of curiosity, be it to see, report, criticize, work, observe or analyse, and a lot of information has been published on the various aspects of that revolution and the US-backed contra attacks into the country.

El Salvador is another story. Although many journalists and 'fact-finding' groups have been in and out of the country since 1980, getting to know the guerrillas who are fighting the US-backed Salvadoran military is not that easy. Neither is it easy to run around the country and simply talk to people to get a sense of what they think in the midst of this war. This is because the military, paramilitary and deathsquad apparatus in El Salvador is something to be feared and, depending on the political climate, it could be a matter of life and death either for the person inquiring or the person responding.

As for material being published on the war, I felt there was little that tried to understand the 'other side'. The exception to this were Raymond Bonner's very interesting reports on the two weeks he spent with the guerrillas for the *New York Times* in 1982, which, to a great extent, cost him his job.

And so, in early 1983, I decided that I wanted to photographically document the guerrillas, their controlled zones[4] and the civilians living in those zones. At that time Reagan was calling them 'terrorists' and our tax monies[5] were (and still are) being used to support, train and advise the Salvadoran military against whom the guerrillas are fighting. I wanted to know who these people were, what they thought, why they were fighting and how they lived.

As for my own qualifications for attempting such a project I felt that since I was born and raised in Latin America, by American parents, I had some understanding of Latin countries. If nothing else I could understand something of the poverty which is usually responsible for all of the turmoil. Growing up in Latin America made me very aware of poverty. It is visually inescapable. Also, because of who my parents are – my mother is a teacher and my father a theologian – I was taught to be concerned with the world around me, to be sensitive to injustice and inequality, to care about those more unfortunate than myself. And so I thought that with my background I could try to cover an aspect of the war in El Salvador, from the guerrilla side, in some depth.

Which brings me to my second reason and a far more personal one: my Latin American past.

I was a teenager when my parents decided to return to the US in the early 1960s. I left a continent that several years later was to explode with a number of repressive and violent military dictatorships. I left behind friends and, to a certain extent, a whole generation of kids, who would shortly confront those dictatorships. Dictatorships are not easily confronted. Consequently all peaceful attempts to question those regimes, to demand political, economic and/or social change, were violently suppressed. This violence, in turn, paved the way for the formation of many different guerrilla groups throughout the continent.

While my generation in America was trying to believe that it could love everybody and, at the same time, was demonstrating against the war in Vietnam, my generation down south, whether participating in a guerrilla movement or not – and the majority did not – was being indiscriminately tortured, killed or simply 'disappeared' because they didn't believe in military dictatorships, or because they didn't believe the majority should be poor, or because they believed in a variety of definitions for the word freedom.

And so I wanted to understand something about how a guerrilla war, the consequence of over 50 years of military dictatorships – as was the case in El Salvador – was lived.

Thus the creation of my project.

Obviously one doesn't choose a project like this and go off and do it. First I had to propose it to the FMLN (Farabundo Martí National Liberation Front),[6] since it was their territory, and get it accepted. Which I did. Three months later I was informed that my project had been approved. But, I was told, I would have to wait until they could organize my entrance into the country and then into their zones. Maybe a month, maybe two. As the months passed, maybe in a couple of weeks, maybe next week. Seven months later I was finally given the OK to go to El Salvador.

Once in the zone I discovered that getting out wasn't going to be that easy either. My planned four months became eleven, and so I lived almost a year in the mountains of El Salvador.

Covering a war from the other side does not provide any of the amenities that the press is accustomed to, such as movability in helicopters or vehicles to go to where something is 'happening' and then get out. Neither does it allow you to go back to the hotel, have a couple of drinks with your own kind, and basically live off and on in the style that you have acquired with such a profession. No. To live fulltime with the other side is hard, and it's lonely.

I don't know of any Western journalist who has spent a year, non-stop, with the Vietcong, the Afghan rebels, the Palestinians or the Eritreans, but after my year with the Salvadoran guerrillas, I think it would be extremely difficult to do. I at least was with Latin Americans, who speak a language I understand and have a history and culture that I know something about, and yet it was still difficult – actually the most difficult year of my life, to date. But to live a year with a people with whom I had no cultural identification would have been, I think, impossible for me.

Here then is my personal account of a year lived with the guerrillas in the mountains of El Salvador. I say personal, because I'm not a historian, political scientist or military strategist. I'm a photographer who lived in a country at war. This is what I learned, experienced, lived; these are the people I met and lived with.

Obviously, I am showing one view of a simple yet complex reality. Simple as poor versus rich, oppressed versus oppressor; complex because human beings, history and wars have never been simple. To understand what is happening in El Salvador many views are needed. What follows is just one of many, just another way of looking.

'For we have been there in books and out of books – and where we go, if we are good, there you can go as we have been' (*Green Hills of Africa* by Ernest Hemingway). This, then, is where I've been.

Map designed by Peter Joseph

Glossary

AMES: Association of the Women of El Salvador

Atlacatl: the most elite battalion of the Salvadoran Government Army

Belloso: an elite battalion of the Salvadoran Government Army

Chile: FPL Command Quarters in Chalatenango

cazadores: common, conscripted, troop battalions

'ears': military and deathsquad spies

Escuelita: guerrilla military school

FDR: Frente Democrático Revolucionario/Democratic Revolutionary Front

FMLN: Frente Farabundo Martí de Liberación Nacional/Farabundo Martí National Liberation Front

FMLN groups: ERP – Ejército Revolucionario del Pueblo/The People's Revolutionary Army

FAL – Fuerzas Armadas de Liberación/Armed Forces of Liberation

FPL – Fuerzas Populares de Liberation/Popular Liberation Force

PRTC – Partido Revolucionario de los Trabajadores Centroamericanos/Central American Revolutionary Workers Party

RN – Resistencia Nacional/National Resistance

gringo/a: US citizen

guinda: evading government forces during an invasion

internationalist: non-Salvadoran usually working in health and/or education

La Una: section of controlled zone in Chalatenango

La Tres: "   "   "   "   "

La Dos: "   "   "   "   "

mara: group or clique

muchachos/chas: boys/girls – civilian term used to describe the guerrillas

Push&Pull: O-2A Spotter Plane – a twin-engine aircraft equipped for visual reconnaissance, target identification and marking, and ground-to-air coordination. Can also fire rockets.

R&R: rest and relaxation

February 1984

OK, throw my knapsack on my back, pick up my camera bag and walk off the plane – just like everybody else. Right? Right. I'm just another photographer coming to El Salvador to cover the war. Yeah, I'm just another, but why am I wearing olive green mountain climbing boots and why such a small knapsack? Nobody asked me anything when my passport was stamped.

As I approached the men at customs with guns tucked into their bellies underneath their shirts I thought, hell, they're not going to let me in. I mean how obvious can I be with my boots, my knapsack with only one change of clothing, 60 more rolls of film and four months' worth of tampax? They only opened my camera bag – just another photographer – and off I went.

So here I am in a little hotel in San Salvador pretending to be someone that I am not, or rather pretending not to be me who is here to do a story on the guerrillas. I've got nothing to do except wait. This time, according to my instructions from three weeks ago, I wait three days and then at a certain time I go to a restaurant and meet *someone*. Great! After the year I spent in New York City with this group – one whole year to get my project approved and to be told when I could go and how – I am not too sanguine about meeting this *someone*. But I've gone this far, so might as well play it out to the end.

Several times in my hotel in Guatemala City – on my way here – I thought, I think I'll catch the next plane to New York. Yes, that's what I'm going to do. I mean, what am I doing here? What am I trying to prove with this project? And the nights are silent in Guatemala City, except for the occasional burst of a machine gun and the screeching of tires and I sit in the dark wondering where I'm going and why.

I've been travelling for six weeks all over Central America getting my passport stamped full of entrances, exits and visas – as I was instructed. In most of these countries I have not known anyone, and where I did have connections I didn't make them, because I can't talk about my project – for security reasons – and so any questions or fears have had to be dealt with by myself with myself as I walk the streets of yet another country, as I sit alone in yet another hotel room.

A friend of mine in New York (one of two people who knew what I was waiting for) told me that my project was going to be difficult, and that by

1

doing it alone it would be even more difficult. But I think that once I get into those mountains things will be all right. I mean this is what I waited a year for, this is what I decided to do, this is what I made happen. I may be scared every once in a while, but all unknowns tend to be frightening and I'm not easily frightened, she said with a stiff upper lip. Oh, I'm tough all right but I have a heart pounding inside that makes it hard to sleep sometimes, and if only someone would put their arms around me and hold me for one night I'd be all right for, at least, another year. But why, why am I doing this?

And the nights steal along the streets of San Salvador nudging the dark windowed, bullet-proof Cherokees[7] concealing men and weapons out on the hunt for humans.

But I know why I'm doing this, why I'm here. I'm here not only because I want to show the American people the other side of this war that we are financing, but also because I need to see, to understand, what this war is all about. What does it mean to fight a guerrilla war? How do you do it, how do you live it? That's what I want to know, how you live it. And so here I am in El Salvador.

I don't believe it! I went to *that* restaurant, at *that* time, and met *that* someone. Ah ha! These people are much better organized than the group up north. Plans are not yet ready for getting me out of the capital and into the mountains, but there seem to be no foreseeable problems, just a matter of a little more time. In the meantime they are concerned with my staying at the hotel and are going to move me to a 'safe house'. Fine with me. I have also been told to come up with a pseudonym. I am, from now on, Taina. It's a Brazilian indigenous name.

I'm staying in a little room at the end of the patio of a small house with another person who is also going to the same front. He, Guillermo, is a radio broadcaster and is going to work with the FPL's[8] radio station, Farabundo Martí,[9] up in Chalatenango. Ana, whose house we are clandestinely staying in, lives with her aged mother and blind father, her nine-year old daughter and four-year old son. Her husband lives elsewhere for security reasons and both are incorporated in the FPL. Ana has been with the FPL for over seven years.

Being cooped up in a little room, without being able to go out, with nothing to read except the daily newspaper, and nothing to do, is a bitch! I thought waiting in New York City was a bitch, not being able to plan anything in my life because I might be leaving tomorrow, or the following week, or the next month; but at least I could run around, read books, see friends, whatever. But waiting in a room, closed off from everything and everyone, is something else. Weeks, we've been here weeks waiting to get out of town. And grandma makes us our meals and either Ana or Renata, her daughter, brings them to our room. Renata comes to visit me almost every day after school. She's a neat kid and I am amazed at her grownupness. She knows that her mother is presently hiding two people who are going to the front, and she says nothing to her school friends.

Ana has been describing the violence that existed in 1978–80 here in the city. One morning she was waiting for a bus with around 15 people. The bus stop was across the street from a park and that morning the park was littered with mutilated bodies with imprints of the 'Mano Blanca' (a notorious deathsquad). She said it was a tactic of the paramilitaries to throw mutilated bodies around town to intimidate the people. As they were waiting for the bus a truck with several National Guards[10] came by and stopped. They jumped out of the truck, divided the group into male and female, frisked everybody and asked for IDs. Then they walked up and down looking at each person. A Guard stopped in front of one man, pointed to him and said: 'Take him.' The man started to protest and the butt of a rifle went in his groin and then in his neck. The Guard continued down the line and pointed to another man. This man also tried to protest and a rifle went down on his head and he collapsed. Another Guard pointed to one more man and a rifle was smashed across his face. They piled the three into the truck and drove off.

According to Ana, throughout 1980 this type of violence, with people being disappeared left and right, was so intense and so pervasive that the FMLN was able to recruit thousands, telling them that they would be given weapons if they went to the mountains. This was the failed general offensive of January 1981. Many people left San Salvador for Guazapa and other areas, but when they arrived in the mountains there was no food and no weapons. The majority returned to the capital, and the massacres and repression increased.

We finally left Ana's house. Guillermo and I were picked up by a truck at a designated place, went downtown where the driver and his friend bought us each a lightweight hammock (when all rolled up it almost fits in the palm of your hand) and a coarsely woven cotton sheet. Then we drove to the outskirts of town. Somewhere we connected with a man waiting for us on the side of a dirt road and he told us that the route we were going to take, to meet up with the people who were to take us to the front, had a military roadblock and so it was not safe to go on. Back to town we went.

With only my toothbrush, I went with one of the men to his home and stayed with his family. Guillermo went with all of our stuff to the other man's house. Three days later we met in a restaurant, got into the truck and drove off. While we were moving I was told what my 'story' was if we got stopped on the way. (When I flew into El Salvador the police gave me only ten days to stay in the country. Therefore I needed to be able to explain what I was doing in the country illegally and why I was travelling in a truck with three Salvadorans.) On the way to wherever we were going we stopped by the side of the road where a woman was waiting and she told us that everything was OK. We drove on, turned on to a dirt road, got to the end of it and waited. But 18:00 hrs came and went and our contact did not appear. The driver became very upset and said that we had to get out of there, so we left. As we crossed a bridge we saw a military truck pulled off to the side of the road and a soldier waving a flashlight. The driver and Guillermo got very nervous. I whispered: 'Hey, cool it guys, he's not stopping us, he's just waving us to go around the truck.' We went on. After a while the driver, who now had a name, Roberto, told us to close our eyes. Ten minutes later we pulled into somewhere and opened our eyes: another house, another room, another batch of people, another wait.

Well, the day after tomorrow we are going to leave again – or try to. I could do with a little walking after being cooped up for almost a month.

March

A little walking? Good God, and we're not even halfway there!

Yesterday we got back into the truck, closed our eyes and drove off. At one point Roberto told us to open them because there was a truckload of people in front staring at us and probably wondering why these two people were sitting with their eyes closed. I agreed.

We went back to the same place. At 18:00 hrs our contact appeared. He picked up my camera bag and said: 'Let's go.' Guillermo and I followed him for about 30 minutes going through several checkpoints manned by armed *compas* (*compa* is short for *compañero/a* and is used to address anyone who is with the FMLN; you do not use this word in the cities as it is a giveaway as to whose side you are on). We arrived at a shack where two men and two women, one with a baby, were waiting – obviously for us.

In New York City I was obsessed with the weight of my knapsack. Nothing extraneous could go into it as I also had a camera bag to carry. I knew I would have to carry everything by myself over difficult terrain.

I bought a kid's knapsack with a metal frame that I could strap my camera bag onto, below, still on the frame, and thus distribute the weight. I knew my bag was going to weigh around 30 pounds, and that was taking a minimum of gear. Therefore my knapsack had to weigh the least possible, and I thought it did, since I packed the least possible.

In the shack everybody started loading up. I strapped my bag to my knapsack and waited until everyone was ready before I put it on my back. I figured I was carrying around 55 pounds, which is half my body weight. The two male *compas* had guns; they were responsible for getting us from San Salvador to Guazapa. We stood in a line, one armed *compa* leading and the other at the rear. The leader said, in a not too friendly voice: 'Nobody talks, nobody makes any noise walking, we are walking through enemy (government controlled) territory, nobody lags behind. Keep up the pace because we have a long way to go.' And off we went.

We walked from 19:00 to 09:00 hrs. The terrain was rugged but not mountainous. We walked on paths, nonpaths, and railroad tracks. We crossed paved roads, crept past government military checkpoints and posts, on and on and on. The pain in my legs and shoulders increased by the hour, then by the half hour, then by the minute. Many times I thought, what am I getting into? What am I carrying this equipment for? To hell with photography! I'm going to dump it all under the next tree and let somebody else be a photographer. At moments I couldn't stand the pain and tears rolled down mixing with the sweat pouring down my face. At 02:00 hrs our guide stopped and said: 'OK, take an hour's rest.'

We crumpled into little heaps on the ground and what seemed like only minutes later a voice said: 'OK, everybody up, time to go.'

Good God, I thought as I stood up, I don't think this body is going to make it. Guillermo came up to me and said: 'You take my knapsack and I'll take yours.'

'Guillermo, my stuff is very heavy.'

'It's all right, I'll take it.'

Under normal conditions I would not have accepted. I believe that one carries one's own weight, always, and if part of the weight is being a photographer one carries what one chooses to be. And I'm tough and I always carry my own weight. But I was too exhausted to be tough and I accepted.

The straps on his pack had busted during the walk so I had to carry it in my arms but it wasn't 60 pounds' worth, just around 35. We walked and the pain got worse. The last two and a half hours I was almost crawling. But it was daylight, we were in guerrilla-controlled territory, near the Guazapa volcano, and so the others let me lag behind. I stumbled along and the *compa* bringing up the rear kept my pace.

Our guide delivered Guillermo and me to the command post and the head *compa* smiled and said: 'Rest.' We found a place under a tree and collapsed.

So, here we are sitting on the side of the Guazapa volcano waiting for our next guide. I am told that higher up the volcano half the area is controlled by government forces and the other half by guerrillas. Further down, towards the valley where I am, the peasants and guerrillas live and move around together. I have eaten bread from a bread co-op, fish from a fish co-op and visited a sugar co-op. The sugarcane comes from a small plantation whose owner fled from the war two years ago. I've seen plots of land where beans, tomatoes and other crops are growing. All of this is done by the community for the community, and the land no longer belongs to anybody, at least while the war is on.

Looking down into the valley it is difficult for me to believe this is a war zone. This front has been bombed daily but not the two days Guillermo and I have been here waiting. A helicopter came by strafing earlier this afternoon. To me it was a curiosity. All of the civilians went running to their bomb shelters, but I wanted to see. There was a *compa* nearby also watching the chopper and so I decided that if it got closer I'd do whatever he did. We stood under a tree and watched, and I couldn't tell what it was strafing as there weren't any people there.

Fear, within the context of war, is an emotion I don't know yet, haven't felt. I had been told that the walk from San Salvador to here was very dangerous, but I didn't sense it; I was so concerned with keeping my legs moving that I didn't have any energy left for fear.

Life here definitely has its own pace. Waited almost a month in San Salvador to get out. Then Monday we walked 15 hours and rested, Wednesday morning we walked 2 and rested, Friday morning 1½, Saturday 6 and here we are resting again. Thank God this is a tiny country. The planes have come and gone and it's very peaceful here – wherever here is.

We spent the night in a bombed-out house with a family living in a room off to the side that was still intact. I was so tired that I strung my hammock badly and my feet were higher than my head – too tired to re-do it, too much pain to sleep, but the night finally went away. At dawn, as we were getting ready to leave, the family came out and I saw a little girl whose head and face were covered in blood. Bats, they said. Jesus!

Late afternoon we headed for a lake which separates one part of Cabañas from Chalatenango – our destination. The walk to the lake was memorable. We walked up and down and higher and higher until we had a magnificent view of the lake and the mountains around and behind it. The sun was setting, the sky was red – it was a postcard shot. Then two A-37s (jet fighter-bombers) came and began to bomb. The earth shook, the bombs echoed, the sky turned redder and I thought, this is surreal. My first war.

The crossing of the lake was also surreal: a full moon, a brightly lit hill on our right – a dam, I was told, and heavily guarded – and there we were in seven aluminum canoes, filled with injured combatants going to hospitals in Chalatenango, silently crossing right in front of them.

On the other side was a mass of people waiting to get across. While I waited for all the confusion to pass I talked to a *compa* and remarked how weird crossing the lake was, with all those lights, almost rubbing elbows with the government forces, and nothing happened. He smiled and told me that a year ago they used to cross the lake in the daytime. One afternoon there were six of them crossing with an internationalist (word for foreigner usually working in medicine or education). As they went around a little inlet they saw another boat approaching. In it were six government soldiers. As the boats got closer the twelve of them raised their M-16s and pointed them at each other. The internationalist covered her head with her hands. They crossed, no one fired, the internationalist raised her head, looked around – the other boat was now behind them – and said: 'I don't understand this war.' The *compa* looked at me, shrugged his shoulders and said: 'That's the way things are.'

The commotion subsided. There were horses to carry the wounded and one to carry our gear.

If I thought the first 15-hour walk was difficult, this one was devastating. This one was all mountains and I wasn't carrying anything!

First we went through government-controlled territory so we couldn't use flashlights, but the moon was out. The mountains got higher. Then we could use flashlights and I pulled out my little weightless one with tiny batteries. That barely lit my path for an hour. Then my guide's batteries died. The moon was gone and I plodded along in the dark trying not to break my feet on the rocks and roots all over the paths. At 04:30 hrs we stopped at someone's house and slept for an hour on their dirt porch; then up and off again.

During this week of walking I had noticed that when you ask a *compa*: 'How much more, how much longer?', they purse their lips, jut out their chin in the direction we are going and say: 'Just over there.'

The sun was coming up and I saw that we were surrounded by mountains. I stopped one of the *compas* and said: 'Wait a minute, *compa*. This time I want to know how many more of these we have to climb. One, three, six more mountains, whatever, but I've got to know because I have to flip another switch in my brain.'

'Only one more, *compita* (diminutive for *compa*), this is the last one we have to climb.'

We were standing in front of one of the highest mountains around. We made it slowly to the top and were taken to a camp.

I imagine the scene from the point of view of the people in the camp: in walked a woman, obviously non-Salvadoran, very thin, bright red arms and face, drenched in sweat and breathing heavily. She stopped in front of a rock, dumped her strange looking knapsack on the ground, sat on the rock, pulled out a cigarette, lit it and stared defiantly around.

Everyone stopped what they were doing and stared at me. I didn't care. I sat, soaking in sweat and smoked my cigarette. After a moment a slender man dressed in fatigues walked over, sat on the ground next to me and said: 'Who are you?'

I looked at him, my eyes getting wider and wider and thought, Oh God no! They're going to send me back to San Salvador because they don't know who I am!

Comandante Douglas, military head of the whole front in Chalatenango, the one who asked me who I was, told me to rest and that he would get back to me later after he checked me out. I flopped into a hammock but was too covered in sweat to sleep so I decided to take a bath. A young girl, one of the cooks in the camp, said she would show me where the bathing area was.

On the way I asked her why she had joined the FMLN. She replied that she had been living in a refugee camp in Honduras with her parents and some of her girlfriends decided to join, so she came along. Not too inspiring an answer, but what the hell. I then asked if this bathing place was just for women; she didn't seem to understand what I meant but said yes. The reason for the question was that all bathing I had done and seen on the way – mostly in rivers – was men and women together with everyone wearing their underwear. My body was covered with flea bites (they seemed to be everywhere since I left the city) and sweat and I wanted to bathe nude.

We arrived at the place: a natural spring coming out of the rocks by the side of the path. The water accumulated in a rectangular rock pool. There were slabs of rocks on one side where two women were scrubbing their clothes. There were stones to stand on next to the pool and a gourd. The idea being that you fill the gourd with water and empty it over your standing body, lather with soap and then rinse yourself.

Since there were no men I decided to take off all of my clothes. I heard one woman scream as I took off my last bit of clothing and when I looked up there was no one there. I must have freaked them out: thin white body all covered with red bites and exposed reddish pubic hair – they ran away at the sight. You never expose pubic hair in rural El Salvador, never. I was too tired to care and proceeded with my bath. Fortunately nobody came by – if I made the women run what would the men have done?

These last eight days have been difficult. The walking and being completely dependent on others for everything. Different people, different houses or camps and now here. It's getting to me. Always the stranger, the outsider. This is a hard world and different from any I've been in. And I've just been in it for eight days. One week! I've got three months to go. I know none of this will be comprehensible without pain, frustration and loneliness. I know.

I sat for an hour talking to an attractive and soft-spoken man. They now knew who I was but didn't know what my project was about. He said he was going to send me to their propaganda house, which would be my base for now, and after I rested I was to write up what I wanted to cover and the time frame, and he would arrange it. As I hoisted my pack on to my back he said: 'If you need anything, someone at the base can get it for you.'

'All I need are cigarettes and a comb.'

He looked at my short hair and laughed, 'You don't need a comb.' Then he handed me half a pack of cigarettes. I was touched – it was the first kind gesture anyone had made towards me since the walk began. I had given away many cigarettes during the walk and at the last camp and not once had anyone offered me one.

At the propaganda house I was shown a hammock to rest in. After a while I heard someone say: 'The coffee is ready and we have sweetbread!' No one invited me. That really hurt. Come on, Taina, cool it, I told myself, and pulled out a cigarette – at least I had cigarettes.

The *Propa* (what everyone calls propaganda) group is made up of 13 fulltime people plus myself. I say fulltime because a number of people seem to come and go through this base. Of the 13 two are children (ages six and ten), one is 14 years old, and the rest are 16 and up, myself being the oldest (36). Two of the guys are ex-combatants who cannot fight anymore as a result of injuries, so they now protect the base and the people who go off to towns to buy paper, ink and other supplies. Two of the young women are the cooks, the 10- and 14-year old are couriers, and the rest work with propaganda in one capacity or another.

The base is a typical peasant handmade adobe house with hard-packed dirt floors. It is located on the side of a mountain, two-thirds of the way up and facing the main path. There are three small rooms and one large one used for working during the day and sleeping at night. Furnishings are sparse, but since this is propaganda, there are a couple of old beat-up tables and chairs. There are a few bamboo makeshift narrow tables where supplies and knapsacks are stored. Except for the washed clothes hanging outside to dry, knapsacks are always packed. Large sections of the roof are missing, but since it's the dry season it doesn't matter; moreover, as most of the houses have few windows, the missing tiles provide very good lighting.

This house is a little more sophisticated than most I've passed through because it has an outhouse. Something I've not seen since being in rural El Salvador. Actually it's not quite an outhouse, just a hole in the ground with a board across and a couple of bushes to give some privacy. But at least the stuff is concentrated in one place. I read Omar Cabeza's *La Montaña Es Algo Más. . .* in Nicaragua, and on the trek from San Salvador to here, I thought of how when he took his first shit in the mountains he grabbed a handful of little leaves and ended up getting shit all over his hand. Well, here it is the dry season and there is little growing. Since living the outdoor life I am always on the lookout for big leaves on the way to the bathroom of my choosing, but the only big leaves I have found are very thin and shiny. Here at *Propa* it's very nice because first, you don't have to tiptoe around the stuff to find a clear space and second, there's lots of blurred mimeographed paper that makes excellent toilet paper.

Another fine aspect to this house is a big cement sink with water flowing in from a hose right in back, facing the patio. A lot of places I've stayed don't have their own water source, so this is a luxury. The water flows into a deep sink and next to it is a slab of cement at an angle to wash clothes on. The deep sink stores the water and you ladle it out with a plastic bowl when washing clothes or yourself.

The only problem is that the sink is right next to the patio, a communal area with long benches against the wall, where people come to rest, chat or work, so it's like bathing in the living room. But I've noticed that Salvadorans don't mind bathing in the living room. Actually bathing is a communal experience, and if someone happens to bathe alone, which is seldom, they will talk to whoever is around at the time. Here most of the women bathe in pairs. They chat away while they leisurely douse themselves, lather and rinse.

As I said, everybody, male and female, wears their underwear when bathing. Fifty per cent of the women wear bras – bare breasts when bathing is no big deal – and a number of them will wear a half slip on top of their underpants. The technique after you're done with your bath is to dry yourself still semi-clothed then wrap the towel around your waist and wriggle out of your wet underpants, men included, then wriggle into a dry pair and on with the jeans or the dress. This ritual is performed every day. I find Salvadorans to be very clean people; they don't feel well if they can't bathe every day. They also thoroughly wash everything they take off.

My procedure is slightly different. For one, I don't bathe every day if I'm just sitting around waiting which is what I've been doing. I'm not dirty, so what's the point? And I still can't get used to dousing myself in cold water or to doing it in the living room. So, I'm shy. And I don't wriggle in and out of my underpants because my towel is too small. I brought a little hand towel because of the weight factor – stupid, but that's what I have and that's what I use. Fortunately both my shirts have long tails so I can be discreet as I shyly turn away from whoever is around and change underpants.

Another daily ritual, of course, is eating. The menu is a plate of beans – in the morning usually cold, left over from the night before – and two tortillas three times a day. The tortillas are not the thin, machine-made ones in Mexico or the small, slightly thicker, machine-ground ones in Nicaragua. These are hand-ground, handmade guerrilla tortillas about six to seven inches in diameter and a good half-inch thick.

There are no utensils, so you break off sections of the tortilla and use it as a spoon, eating the spoon and pulling off another piece until you're finished. Then you take your plastic plate to where the water is – plastic jug, spout or river – wash it and hand it in for the next person. Everybody washes their plate.

This was one of the first things I noticed in Guazapa and I was very surprised. Even if you eat in a civilian's house you always wash your plate – it's the code of the guerrillas.

The beans are cooked in water, with some salt, in big pots over wood-burning fires. The large dried kernels of corn are boiled in water and lye in huge pots or cans. When cooked they are washed over and over again. If it's a FMLN camp there is usually a small metal hand grinder clamped on to a piece of wood where I have seen male *compas* taking turns grinding the corn. This coarsely ground corn is then ground a second time by the cooks, all female and very young, on a special stone slab using a long oval stone in their hands. Grinding the corn between stones is all wrist work. As the dough is ground on the stone the cook divides it into balls, which she places in a bowl. Another cook places a ball in the palm of the her hand and slaps it as she turns it with both hands until it is a tortilla. This is then dropped on to a metal sheet lying over a hot wood-burning fire. When one side is done they have a technique of slapping their palm on to the uncooked side, and then flipping it on to the other side. When cooked they stack them in piles. Depending on the number of people the piles get quite high. Tortillas always seem to be made fresh for each meal, so if the beans are cold at least the tortillas are hot.

I have never much liked tortillas. In Nicaragua when I was out in the countryside I refused them. Here I have very little choice: hunger or tortillas. So I eat them but only one at a meal. The cook handing out the food always says, 'You can have two, take two.' I only take one and she looks at me strangely.

Being near the equator the days and nights are fairly well divided – twelve hours each. *Propa* has an allotment of candles so there is a glow after the darkness begins. But not for long. Then everybody to bed. Bed, for the majority, is the ground, inside or out. Mostly inside. As with bathing, most have company when sleeping on the ground. Depending on the night, there may be 8–15 of us sleeping in the room.

When it gets dark you take your plastic and sheet out of your knapsack and lay the plastic on the ground, take off your boots – if you have them – or your rubber flipflops, lie down with all of your clothes on and cover yourself with the sheet. You tuck the sheet tightly around your feet, all around your sides and behind your head. You are, literally, tucked in – like a mummy.

The reason for being so tucked in is because of the bats. With everything covered it's more difficult for them to bite. I'm told that they are more prone to bite those sleeping on the ground than those in hammocks because it's easier for them. The process goes like this: they lick the place where they are going to bite, their saliva is an anesthetic and a de-coagulant; they bite and you don't feel it; the blood runs freely and they sit there and lick it up. Charming, absolutely charming. Why is there such a problem with vampire bats? (Most places around here seem to have both the seed eating and the vampire ones.) Because over the last four years the majority of domestic animals have been killed by the government forces during invasions, thus the bats that normally drink animal blood drink human blood.

Tucking myself in while lying in a little nylon hammock is quite a dance. Getting used to this little hammock is going to take some time. So last night I decided to go sleep outside, on the ground, with several other *compas*. There was a three-quarter moon, the sky was full of stars and the silence was profound. This is a war zone? As an outsider it is still difficult to comprehend.

Carlos, head of *Propa*, said that it was difficult for him and other *compas* who worked in the cities or outside El Salvador when they first came to the front. 'Theory is theory', he said, 'but it is only through living the war, in the zones, with the peasants and the guerrillas that one can understand it.' I don't yet, but I hope to.

There is coffee today for everyone. Great! While waiting for our bean and tortilla breakfast (for some reason they cook further down the mountain and bring up our meals) I heard this conversation:

'If the Marines invade our country I want an M-16 so I can kill them,' said a young woman.

'It's the bomber planes that frighten me. If the Marines come on the ground, that's all right, I have no problem fighting them on the ground. It's the bombs that I don't like,' said a 14-year old boy.

'What I'm afraid of is that when we start fighting the Marines there won't be any food and we'll all go hungry,' said the same woman.

'Hungry? Hell, we've been hungry all our lives. We've got no problem with hunger,' responded another man.

I am still waiting for my project to begin. I found out that the kind fellow I met is *comandante* Esteban, second-in-command of the FPL and responsible for me. Seems like everyone has someone responsible for them, or better put, someone above them. Mine's a top honcho. I'm glad. But why hasn't he gotten back to me?

Chalatenango, locally called Chalate, is one of the largest and poorest states in El Salvador. The area is mountainous and the land rocky. The FPL began organizing the peasants here in the early 1970s for two reasons: because the area was abandoned by the government and was full of peasants, and because it had mountains, and in the manuals of guerrilla warfare you must have mountains: Chalate *is* mountains.

El Salvador has the highest concentration of people per square mile in all of Central America. Yet during my walks I have seen few people and few houses. I have not walked through the fertile areas such as Usulután (the breadbasket of El Salvador) but the areas I have seen seem empty, the vegetation sparse, the land rugged and hard.

The worst repression here in Chalate was from 1977–9. The last major government invasion was in November 1982 when 15,000 soldiers swept through the area. The *compas* were on the run for many weeks, there was little food and most were barefoot. (To be on the run or to evade the government forces during an invasion is called a *guinda*.) After that invasion there was a small one in August 1983 and a smaller one in February, just before I entered the front. It seems that the Salvadoran military is not that interested in this zone, for the moment. The zone is now the rearguard of the FMLN: weapons, ammunition and other materiel are buried in many underground storage areas throughout these mountains; battalions operating in other fronts come here for R&R; and more sophisticated and secure hospitals are located here.

Carlitos, a 16-year old ex-combatant in the FPL's elite battalion and now, because of injuries, a security person here at *Propa*, told me about his family.

His father worked for *Orden* (a famous deathsquad) and was killed by the guerrillas. His two older brothers are government soldiers. One of them became a lieutenant after shooting their mother through the head because she sympathized with her younger son who was/is a guerrilla.

Rene, a 14-year old courier, has no family. They were killed by the government forces right in front of him.

The families of a lot of kids fighting here have been totally or partially wiped out by the war or are divided. For many their family is now the FMLN. A *compa* I met in Guazapa told me that when he is given time off he has nowhere to go, no family to visit.

Then there are the younger kids, the children, who, surrounded by war, have only the armed *compas* to identify with and an 'enemy' to hate. Makes me sad. There is little else inside their heads. The cool thing will be to have a gun someday. What an environment, first poverty and now war.

These people without arms, without mothers, lovers, husbands, living in a rugged and difficult environment. What sacrifice – no? But maybe for these peasants this is not such a sacrifice, maybe this is my middle-class background reacting. I bitch about eating beans and tortillas day-in and day-out because it's not my world. How can peasants bitch about that which is all they know, which constitutes their world?

I finally got out of the base today and walked for three hours to Tamarindo, a hamlet of about 350 people. I have no sense of direction when walking in this area. It's just all mountains to me, and bare ones at that, since this is still the dry season (November through April). The narrow paths that interconnect this world wind up and down and around, and one mountain looks the same as another. Obviously, I am not a mountain person.

I went to Tamarindo to photograph the municipal elections. In this area of the controlled zone the civilians who are with the FMLN have created their own government called Popular Power. Every six months they hold municipal elections when people vote for their local president and three others, in charge of production, defence, and health and education. The area is divided into seven localities, each locality representing five to seven hamlets. Then once a year these 28 locally elected representatives vote for the sub-regional *junta* which is responsible for the overall coordination and administration of the localities. It is called sub-regional because Popular Power originated in and developed from this area which is only a section of the controlled zone. I find it amazing that these people have created their own government whilst fighting a war.

Many of the people living in Tamarindo as well as in the other hamlets are not from this particular area or even state. They have come here fleeing from the repression in their own towns and from fear of the deathsquads and the National Guard. Thus the houses they are living in are not theirs. The owners themselves have fled from the war.

Most of the houses show signs of some form of destruction from bombs, mortars or whatever the soldiers managed to do during one of their sweeps. If there is one room still livable in a house there is one family living in it, rather large families as these are Catholic peasants. If there are two or three rooms livable in a house, then there are two or three families living there and they share a hearth outdoors where they make their beans and tortillas.

I am told that no one fixes up their houses because of the bomber planes. When you hear one coming you check the fire to see if it's smoking and you put it out if it is, and you bring in any clothes hanging on the trees to dry, pretending that this is just another bombed out house with no one in it.

Elections were held in a small school. It consisted of a large blackboard with seven names listed. To the right was a space to make a small vertical line with a piece of chalk. Each voter could vote for a president and three others. Since most were illiterate, someone read off the names and they would make their chalk mark next to the ones they wanted.

After the elections they had a dance to celebrate. I stayed over and slept on the ground and was bitten non-stop by fleas. I must learn to take my hammock and sheet wherever I go – this sleeping on the ground is too painful with all of my bones and too flea ridden. But it's the walking that bothers me more than the ground. My feet hurt like hell because of the corns I have on each little toe; they rub against my boots and it's painful. I should have had them cut out before I came.

Walking back to my base I developed a new mentality called 'Zen and the art of walking.' So far it means: time is of no importance, I do not look ahead at the mountains I must climb, I stare at the path, moving one foot ahead of the other in a rhythmic blank.

I've been in this front 11 days and it's still hard to sense that there is a war going on. Without talking to the people living in these hamlets and ignoring the condition of their houses, you would think this was just another poor, rural Central American place. You wouldn't know that the land and the houses don't belong to anyone now, that the bits of furniture and pots and pans have been scavenged from other bombed out places, that these people have a past full of war and death and fleeing and living out of knapsacks, just like the guerrillas.

There is so much to learn, to understand, and all I want is a piece of sweetbread! I remember when I first got here and saw people pouring sugar down their throats, I thought, my God, people, you're going to ruin your teeth and it's bad for your bodies! Ha! I'm doing the very same thing. My body craves sugar, I don't know why but it does.

I have just met someone called Julio who is not a peasant. Actually he's from my own class and working in the same field. He is temporarily staying in a house just down the mountain, waiting until the photo and film *mara*

(Salvadoran word for group or clique) is reorganized. I'm learning a number of things from him as he's been photographing the war for over three years.

The first thing I have learned and very important to know, is how to make coffee here in these mountains: get a can, fill it with water, put it on the fire, when it starts to boil throw in the ground coffee and let it boil a couple of seconds, take it off the fire, the grains fall to the bottom, pour it into a cup, pour in lots of sugar and you have a superb cup of coffee.

'But where do you get the coffee Julio?'

'Ask Soila, who has the little store down the mountain, to get some in Zapotal. She'll toast it and grind it for you.'

Which I've done and now I have coffee, sugar and, of course, cigarettes. What more could one wish for in life?

One of the things I became aware of immediately here in the front is that those who have money, a minority, buy things just for themselves. They don't share except, maybe, with their best friend. I thought a guerrilla movement would share everything. It makes me very uncomfortable to have things when others do not, but this is the way they do it and I will too, but only to a certain extent, for goods such as coffee, sugar, cigarettes and sometimes bread. When I have bread I try to eat it discreetly because I feel terrible eating in front of others. But the people here at *Propa*, who have food, don't seem to care if they eat right in front of the others. You should see those hungry eyes. And why not? I don't know, the lack of sensitivity here makes me very uncomfortable. I have the feeling that I'm the only one around here who feels this way. This is another world and I must be patient with it.

Francisco, a doctor who has been working in the front lines for over two years, came by to visit Julio. He is on sick leave and may have to leave the country; there is something wrong with his liver, but no one knows what. We spent the evening drinking coffee and I listened to war stories.

Some time ago Francisco was in the Guazapa front working in a hospital when a couple of A-37s came by and began to bomb. Everyone went running off to the bomb shelters. One woman, eight and a half months pregnant, couldn't run fast enough and was killed. Minutes later Francisco reached her, performed a caesarean and took out a live baby. Death and life simultaneously.

Well, here I am living in a controlled zone in El Salvador in the middle of a war and I'm bored. Hell. The problem is that I'm still waiting to hear from Esteban so I can start my project, plus the people here at *Propa* are not very interesting, so it's no fun talking to them. Watching them I get a sense that they don't have strong likes and dislikes, they don't seem to care much either way. Perhaps this is a luxury they can't afford. Perhaps this is just my character. They move along slowly, day after day, laughing, talking, working a little, but nothing they do is excessively profound; they are not complicated creatures.

Carlos says anytime I want to send a message to Esteban – which I've just done – he'll have it sent to the *Chile*, the name of the high command where Esteban operates from. The mail service here seems to function well. If it's local it's taken by ten or twelve-year olds, if it's further away but still in the daytime it's taken by older boys, if it's very far and at nighttime it's taken by men. There are drop-off points in certain camps if a letter is being sent to another front and on it goes. Notes are written on small pieces of paper, folded into one-inch squares, stapled or taped, and with to and from written on one side.

At least Julio is interested in my project and has the time to work on some of it with me. We have decided to go to Los Amates, by the Sumpul River, to photograph a small vegetable and fishing cooperative.

Julio, Francisco and I walked five and a half hours this morning to Los Amates. The minute we got there we bumped into a group from the *escuelita* (little school, the name for military training schools). They said that there were government forces just over the river, that they were going to be leaving soon and so should we. We ate the usual and walked back. On the way we decided to spend the night in Tamarindo. Just before we got there Francisco stopped in front of a big tree with an uneven stone platform next to it. He said that in 1979 the government soldiers, pretending they were *compas*, yelled to all the town folk that they had to go to a demonstration in San José de las Flores – a now-deserted larger town, 20 minutes from Tamarindo. About 40 people started walking down the path. The soldiers told them to stand under the tree and shot them down.

I'm back at the base after walking 13 hours in the last two days, and I didn't photograph any production. Most production is going to be impossible to shoot as it's the dry season – nothing is growing. They will only plant in May, with the first rains, and then it needs time to grow and I won't be here. Then there is the problem that we are in a war and nothing can be scheduled with any certainty. Problems, problems and time is passing.

I don't think my project is viable. The only way to do what I want is to stay here a year. Time in this place does not acknowledge calendars or watches. What I want is too vast and was projected without knowing this world. So what am I to do? Here comes another plane. . .

I must rethink my whole project and discuss it with Julio. Thank God for Julio and now Francisco. For the first time in 40 days, just counting the time I've been in the country, I have people I can talk to.

Reconnaissance planes buzzed around all last night and this morning. Government elections[11] are going to be held tomorrow. Last night Carlos came back at midnight and woke everybody up to tell us to prepare for a bombing attack early in the morning. He was nervously grabbing notebooks and other papers off the tables and handing them to Elena, telling her to put them in a bag – why can't *he* put them in the bag? Anyway, I shrugged in my hammock and said, 'The country is too full of international press and observers. The last thing they are going to do is bomb the countryside on election day. Wouldn't look good.' Carlos mumbled back something about wanting to see me with my boots on at 05:00 hrs. At 05:30 I was brushing my teeth, Carlos was not around and life proceeded as usual. Either I'm completely out of it or something clashes with me in this house.

It is 07:00 hrs and I've got a tin of coffee on the fire under a tree – my new spot these days. It's a cloudy day, the first I've seen in El Salvador. No planes today I bet. The house is behind me with everybody yelling and screaming. There is no silence here except when they are sleeping in the afternoon. Oh well, I'm happy; I've got my coffee and thoughts to think about.

Going back to the idea of several days ago about sacrifice, or about how I can't stand eating beans and tortillas three times a day; the more I see how people live here in these mountains the more I ask myself how do they do it, because I find life here incredibly difficult. There is no electricity, there are no toilets, no phones, no roads, no vehicles. To go anywhere you go by foot, up and down winding mountain paths. Transporting goods is done on your back or on your head. Working the land is done by hand with the aid of a circular machete. There are no fertilizers, tractors or irrigation. Bathing is done in a river or at a communal spout. And because there are so many stones everywhere, because we wash our clothes on stones, because we eat tortillas ground on stones, I have the feeling, at times, that we are living in the stone age. Except for airplanes and radios there is no indication that we are even in the nineteenth century let alone the twentieth!

And it's beginning to hit me that for the majority of the people here, living and fighting a war under these conditions, this is no sacrifice because this is the way they've been living for years! Possibly centuries. It's brutal and it's hard and it's poor, Jesus, it's poor. I've given up my world to live here but they, they are living in theirs.

Another thing I feel is that the peasants here in the controlled zones have a sense of dignity. They are not ashamed of their poverty, nor are they servile in the way many poor in Latin America can be. Something about fighting in this war in whatever way – be it growing food for the combatants – makes these people proud and dignified.

Going back to the kids and how I get upset because all they have are guns and war; I think it is like my thoughts on sacrifice – I need to perceive things differently. What kind of hope or future does poverty offer? What kind of role models did these kids have before the war? For most of us middle-class Americans are uncomfortable with war, with the violence of war. But what about the violence of poverty? I've only been here two weeks but I'm beginning to understand that poverty is a violent way of life.

War tableau: during a *guinda* Julio, Toño (another FMLN photographer), an old man and a kid are last in a long line. They hear people moving behind them and think it's the enemy so they get into a group: Julio pointing his pistol, Toño holding out his knife, the old man lifting his machete and the kid holding a stick. There they stand waiting for the enemy. The people coming behind are *compas* – stopping in front of this dramatic group they ask: 'What the hell do you all think you're doing?'

Julio and I spent several days in Tamarindo. The first day we photographed a military hospital. There was a bit of a row when we arrived because the two doctors and the nurse, all three internationalists, wanted to know who I was and whether I had been cleared to shoot. They all knew Julio. Julio got indignant and said that I had complete clearance, that I was not the typical journalist, that I was going to be living here for several months, that *comandante* Esteban had okayed the hospital, and how much higher did they want to go?

Then they said that they couldn't be photographed. I said that I wouldn't photograph their faces. 'Ah!' they said, jumping up and down, 'that's what every photographer says but they all lie.' Julio got angrier, the Salvadorans couldn't figure out what everyone was getting upset about, and finally we made peace.

The hospital was located in a typical adobe house. There were two rooms, one with six rustic beds and a few hammocks, and the other, a smaller one, was the operating room. There were more hammocks and beds on a veranda facing the inner patio. Several injured combatants were lying around. One who had recently had his leg amputated from the knee on down was being washed in the patio by three giggling young women.

The operating room had two open doorways and part of the roof missing. The operating table was a wooden door raised to the right height.

One of the doctors was preparing to perform an operation. He wore pants, mountain climbing boots and no shirt. It was humorous to see him putting on a white apron, gloves and surgical mask over a half naked body. It was also interesting to see them unwrap the sterilized surgical instruments from newspapers. I was told that it didn't matter what you wrap them in but how you sterilize them. These wrapped instruments had been placed in tin cans and then sealed, then placed inside a larger can and then on the fire for the required time.

Just before starting the operation I asked the doctor if I should wear a mask while I photographed. He laughed and said, 'What's a few more bacteria with all of these door and roof openings?'

I was very impressed. They had anesthesia, glucose, IVs, and a doctor cutting open a body in a mud hut.

As Francisco told me, they have come a long way since 1980. Even in 1982 and 1983, when many times they had no anesthesia and few surgical implements, they were performing incredible operations. Francisco prides himself for rarely performing amputations during those years.

The military hospital in this area is moved every month or so for security reasons. People are captured and talk, others leave and talk, and if the government forces know of the location of a hospital they bomb it as quickly as possible.

Julio and I stayed at the local president's house, a gathering point for the hamlet. It's a three-room house and therefore full of people.

I spoke to a couple of women living there who were grinding corn. Two years ago they left their houses in the town of Chalatenango, capital of this state. 'When we were still in our houses' is a reference to another time. One told me that three of her brothers were killed by deathsquads and one disappeared. In her mother's family all are dead except for a brother. Five of this brother's kids were killed by the government forces and now only three are left, two of whom are government soldiers. It seems to be always the same story: death in the family and families divided.

I asked them about the elections. One of them started talking about their own elections and I said I meant the government elections. 'Oh, those, I don't know.' A complete lack of interest. I asked the other one if she had voted in the government elections in 1982.

'No, I felt too embarrassed.'

'Embarrassed, why?'

'Because there were so many people.'

Oh, thinks I, I see. . . These are very simple folk.

Going back to our base Julio and I stopped for a rest. On the side of the mountain we saw an old couple clearing the dried land with their hands and a circular machete; that view could have been seen, I imagine, years before photography was invented. We walked over to them. The man was 69 years old and his wife slightly younger. They were preparing the land for planting. They pointed to a plot across the mountain that AMES, a women's organization, was getting ready to plant for the widows of the war in this area.

The man told us that he had been with the FPL for 13 years, and that in the beginning of the war, when they didn't have any guns, he and four others made guns out of wood because at night they looked real. With these wooden guns they attacked a small military post and got a real gun, then they attacked another one and so forth. That's how they got their first weapons.

'If we had the guns then that we have now the enemy would be finished,' said his wife.

'Now, I'm too old to fight', he said, 'so I grow food for the *muchachos*.' (Boys – word often used when referring to the guerrillas.)

They have had 26 children.

'When we got back from burying one, there was another one dead,' he said. 'Now, we have ten left. But none of them live with us. They are all fighting and on their own – we couldn't afford to feed them.'

I asked him what he thought of the government elections.

'Elections? Never voted in my life. With elections, without elections, with a government, without a government, our needs are never represented, there is never any concern for us. Nothing changes – we still wake up hungry.'

They were so thin, so old and yet their smiles expressed strength and purpose.

Continuing our walk Julio said he believed that the guerrillas were the true hippies: they live communally, their drug is the revolution, they share everything and they have a great love for peace. I don't know about all of those but it definitely is a communal existence and there is no 'mine' except for what's in your knapsack.

April

The birds are chirping in my study of trees and mountains and it's another morning in El Salvador. At times I feel that I'm not really living in that country, but here I am.

I spent the evening with Karla (an internationalist), Benito (a doctor), Julio and Toño. We talked about war, history, philosophy, technology – all kinds of things. Everyone was full of energy and intensity, especially Benito, who seemed hungry for talk and ideas. Toño told one of his favorite stories:

He had recently arrived in the Guazapa front, two years ago, and had to take a shit. He picked up a book and went off to look for a secluded spot. Upon finding one he squatted down, opened his book and started to read. No sooner had he started to shit when he heard some noise and looked up. A column of about 50 guerrillas was marching towards him. He mumbled 'Oh no!', but there was nothing he could do, so he stayed where he was and, turning bright red, stared intently at his book. The column passed.

Toño is a tall, slender, bearded fellow with sparkling eyes, and he lives, breathes, dreams filmmaking, and feels almost as passionately about everything else in life. He looked at us laughing and said, 'You know, living this way, doing these things, giving one's life, you've got to be a little crazy, no? We're all fucking crazy!'

'Yes, yes, we're all humanly crazy!' Benito roared back.

As I was about to go up to my base to sleep Benito said, 'It's so rare to spend time talking like this. There just aren't many people with whom one can talk about these things.' I guess I'm not the only one who thinks this.

The short walk up from Julio's was beautiful: a full moon and a mist over the mountains. Truly beautiful and so quiet. Julio says if you look closely at the full moon it is a mirror wherein Chalate is reflected.

I went to Zapotal with some people from *Propa*. It's one of those towns where the people living in it aren't necessarily with the FMLN, but it's in the controlled zone and they are there because that is where they live and have their little stores, etc.

The walk to town was very pretty. First we climbed the remainder of the mountain we live on, then over and around until we got to a road. A road! You can actually see where it was cut out of the side of the mountain many years ago. Now it's covered with rocks and weeds and has not been used except by the FMLN since 1982. Now it's their road, their land.

The view from the road was spectacular, mountains everywhere. It's hard for me to imagine, coming in 1984, that all of these mountains and the ones I can't see are all in a controlled zone and that each one of them has been the scene of one bloody battle or another in the history of the war. These mountains that sit humped rather lazily in the heat of the noon sun. What war? Turning the bend I could see the Sumpul River winding around – itself the scene of several major massacres. Then on the other side, Honduras, just more mountains.

Zapotal was just as Julio described it: any moment you expect to see Don Quixote riding on Rocinante coming around the corner; rock roads, stone walls, thick adobe, tiers of firewood, all blending into a solid texture.

The type and quantities of merchandise sold in the little stores really shows the poverty of this region. You can buy nickle, dime or quarter packets of instant coffee, spaghetti, margarine, crackers, etc. They sell little tubes of toothpaste, tiny bottles of shampoo, little notebooks; and pills are sold individually. Yet when buying beans and corn it is done by the sackful; and rice, sugar and salt are sold by the pound.

For a bean-tired photographer everything looked fantastic. I bought four eggs and sweetbread. What luxury! I could have bought many other things, and wanted to, but I'm still having a very difficult time with the if-you-have-money-you-buy-and-keep-it-to-yourself mentality. Except for cigarettes, coffee, sugar and bread when available. I give a number of cigarettes away daily so I don't feel too bad about that. My coffee and bread, except down at Julio's – to hell with it – it's in the morning when I'm in my office under the tree writing. I think, by now, everybody at *Propa* is used to me sitting out there and they know that it's still difficult for me to face beans and tortillas for breakfast.

I taped a long interview with Rutilo, a priest, on the Christian participation and involvement in the war. He's a very warm, big and energetic man, in his early forties. He wears a big black hat which someone gave him, a safari shirt, and a gun and holster belted around his waist. He told me that the gun was not his idea. One day a couple of years ago, after giving mass in a town, a small group went up to him and handed him the gun and holster pleading with him to wear it as he is constantly on the move, going all over the place, and many times has had very close encounters with the government forces.

He started out by giving me the history of Church, State and Peasant of El Salvador, beginning with the colonizers. I got a long history.

In the last four years in El Salvador we have been writing our own Bible, similar to the Bible of the Jews. But we must not forget that the Bible is the history of a people yet each people have their own history and consequently their own Bible. And the Bible of one people cannot be used to negate the Bible of another. Nicaragua has its own Bible, its own Moses Sandino. We have our Bible and our Moses Farabundo . . . I see the Salvadoran government, the US government, those who oppress our people, they are thick like an arm. The people are weak like the pinky but this little finger is much more agile and can move faster and has not only escaped annihilation but has now, in 1984, created its own organizations here in the zones . . . In 1932 the government killed 30,000 peasants, in this recent chapter they have killed over 40,000. The people finally saw the necessity of creating their own army and now have created their own government, which I believe expresses their desire for peace.

Esteban came by. What a surprise! We talked about my project, schedule and getting out. He told me that bullets have four sounds: (1) when you can hear the shots back and forth – they are far away; (2) when you can hear them whistle by – they are closer; (3) when they no longer whistle but whisper; and (4) when there is no sound, just the movement of air next to your body – these are meant for you.

I spent the evening down at Julio's. Lots of coffee and war stories again. Benito was there and a couple of old-time combatants, meaning they have been through many years of the war and all of the changes.

Julio and Lucas, an explosives expert, tell the story of something that happened to them a couple of years ago: they are attacking a town, everything is going well. Lucas is told to blow up a particular house, which is a headquarters of something or other. He sends out his team to pack the explosives. When they are ready the idea is to storm the place after it blows up. Julio is also there with a movie camera waiting to film. He holds the camera to his eye, the *compas* are ready to move in and Lucas says, 'OK!' The *compas* move in closer and nothing happens. This happens three times and Julio, who can't hear anything, starts the camera whenever the *compas* move in, but then they stop and move back. 'Like seeing a movie in reverse,' he says. Finally on the third try: boom! The house explodes, the *compas* move in. The problem is that they wired the wrong house, the one next door, and there stand a little old couple, surrounded by rubble and wondering what happened to their house. When the battle is over they go and apologize to the couple and find them another house to live in.

We laugh and laugh and Lucas is hysterical, waving his hand that now only has one finger left on it. Then someone else tells a story. Benito fiddles with the radio and finds a classical station. It is playing Mozart and Benito hums along. He has a trained voice and knows the music well. Here we are in the mountains, in the midst of a war, a plane comes, we blow out the candles, the plane goes, we light them again, and Benito sings Mozart. Sometimes I forget, sometimes I can't see it, sometimes it seems like a dream. I am told the story of a war and am living one level of it.

I went back to Tamarindo so I could attend and photograph the annual sub-regional elections. It was a two-day affair. As I mentioned earlier the 28 locally elected representatives voted for the sub-regional *junta* made up of five people: president, vice-president, and three others in charge of production, defense, and education and welfare.

Present at the elections were the 28 voters and a number of others invited to attend but without voting rights: the *Estado Mayor* (Chiefs of Staff), the *Comité Zonal* (political head of the FPL), AMES (Association of the Women of El Salvador), CONIP,[12] a few others and myself, the only foreign observer.

María, the incumbent president, was in charge and began the affair by going over the agenda for the next two days. She then gave a long and detailed account of what had been happening on the international scene. This lasted for over two hours, with many questions. A *compa* stood and asked for permission to take a pill; permission was granted by all. Three *compas* arrived late and had to account for their delay; excuses were accepted by all.

María then shifted to the national scene. She analysed the economic, social, political and military situation in the country.

After lunch each incumbent *junta* member gave a detailed report on the successes and failures in their areas. A *compa* asked permission to attend to biological needs; permission was granted by all. The reports took up the rest of the afternoon.

What these people have accomplished and what they have tried and failed to do just in the last six months is very impressive. More so when you consider that they are peasants, many illiterate, underfed, doing all kinds of jobs, fighting a war and developing their own government.

The following morning María passed out mimeographed sheets with the government's program: introduction, general objectives, specific objectives, and one and a half pages of means and ways of implementing or expanding them. We were divided into groups of 12 and the groups dispersed under the trees to discuss the sheets.

I went off with a group and listened for two hours. Again, all I can say is I was impressed. One *compa* who could read, slowly read the first item for discussion. They went around the circle allowing each person to give his opinion (the group I was with were all male). Each of them had an opinion, actually several. Often times one would say almost the same thing as the other one but they all wanted to speak. In the first half hour they had only gotten through three items and there were 30 yet to go through. Finally a *compa* said, 'Wait a minute, at this rate we'll never get through half. We have to organize ourselves better.'

'I've got an idea', said another *compa*. 'We read each item, someone talks, if we agree with him we don't all need to talk unless we want to add something.' Everybody agreed.

This group was very vocal and sometimes they just couldn't contain themselves and had to give their opinion even when it was a repetition. But they were conscious of this and tried to keep things under control. They didn't get through the whole list but it was fascinating to watch them organize themselves more and more as time went by.

The reason I was fascinated was that from what I know of the history of El Salvador, I don't think these peasants voiced an opinion in a group five years ago. I don't think they were ever asked what they thought about a government, much less asked to participate in one and one that represents their needs and interests. And they take their government seriously, they get involved in it with gusto – it's like an enormous hunger to learn, to grow, to participate in a process that is theirs.

During lunch the *Estado Mayor* arrived with Cmte (abbreviation for *comandante*) Leonel Gonzalez, top *comandante* of the FPL, Cmte Esteban, their respective aides, and the *Comité Zonal* arrived with Cmte Susana and her entourage.

After lunch a person from each of the morning discussion groups reported. (These reports will be studied by the new *junta*.) Then the elections were held. On a blackboard in the front of the group were written eight names. Those who could vote stood up, one at a time, and voted for five names.

After the voting Leonel gave a short speech ending with: 'You are participating in the battle as much as the military because without you, without Popular Power, there is no reason to fight this war. You represent the advancement of our people in our struggle to create a new way of life.'

Then there was an open discussion between the people and the *comandantes*. This also was very interesting. As I said, these people have opinions and want to state them. They did it shyly at first but they were not intimidated when speaking to the *comandantes* even when they were being critical.

One man said, 'The *muchachos* should have more respect for the civilians and especially for the Popular Power reps. When they get time off and come to one of our bases they should report to the nearest rep to say how long they will stay and show their permission to be on leave so that we know it's a real *compa* and not an infiltrator.'

Leonel agreed and said they would work on it.

Another stood up and said, 'One thing that really angers me is that a *compa* comes and spends the night and during the night he'll shoot off his gun to show off. We don't like that – our children are already traumatized by the bombings – we don't like to hear guns going off for nothing.'

Esteban agreed completely. They had heard this complaint several times and had spoken about it to the troops. He would bring it up again.

I liked the interaction between the two groups. It was one of mutual respect. Not only did the *comandantes* reply to the questions and complaints but they reported on some of the things they were thinking and working on militarily.

The elections are over. The Popular Power house is finally quiet and I'm tired. These last two days have been heavy. Trying to take in everything, note down everything and take pictures.

I fart, he farts, we all fart – the farting guerrillas. But what do you expect from a diet of beans? What amazes me is that I haven't gotten sick yet. The places I've drunk water from. . . Actually, I'm better off than most because I'm taking anti-malaria pills. Most people here get malaria, suffer for a week, then it's over until the next time. Even Julio. He prefers to get malaria five or six times a year to taking anti-malaria pills for years. They're bad for you. I know, but I'm still taking them.

I interviewed María, the former sub-regional president. She's a peasant from Chalatenango, in her early thirties and short and plump. She walks all over the zone with her 11-year old daughter – they are quite a team. She has two older daughters, one a nurse, the other a radio person in a battalion in another front.

She has been politically active since 1972. I asked her if it was difficult to go from organizing and demonstrating to picking up a gun. What brought her to that point?

I think that life itself – the way we live – brought us to this point. Look, when I belonged to the FTC (Federation of Rural Workers) we workers would go on strike demanding an increase in salary and rice, beans and tortillas for lunch. Those in power would send in the National Guard and they would beat us up, kill some of us, capture and disappear others. This is the way we lived. After so much violence and repression you decide that the enemy doesn't understand words. You have to go to war against him because he forces you to. If you ask for something they kill you, if you join a union or an organization they kill you. Finally we organized in order to defend ourselves and as we grew and developed we defended ourselves offensively, not defensively. When you live with this type of violence you learn quickly that the enemy is really out to get you, to annihilate you, to pull you out by the roots. And that is what I mean when I say life – the way we live – teaches us, makes us commit ourselves to another way of fighting so much violence. Look what they did to Monsignor Romero (Archbishop of San Salvador, assassinated by paramilitaries while giving a sermon in 1980), a gentle, humble and peaceful man – and rrrras! (her sound for a bullet) they killed him. Only bullets frighten the enemy; only an armed struggle can end this situation. And it is a decision that you make because life has taught us, daily, that this is what we have to do. I remember in the beginning of the war, we had a few pistols and some wooden rifles. When I did nightwatch I had four little firecrackers in my hand – at least it startled the enemy and woke up the *compas* and gave us time to run. And now we have mortar, 120-mm cannons, and machine guns.

I asked her the difference between living here before they had controlled zones and after.

I think living in the zone opens your eyes, teaches you about the reality you live in, while in the past, with all the terrible domination, you never could figure out or explain anything. I think there is a great difference. On the other hand, it is true that then we didn't have the anguish of the bomber planes or of invasions, but there were repressive forces, the National Guard, the police, the deathsquads, that controlled everybody's life. Nobody could say anything! Absolutely nothing! Now we have land to cultivate and I won't say that we eat better than before, no, we live in a war and during invasions the enemy kills any domestic animals they find and destroys our food. But as the war advances, our people living in the zone live better and better. In 1981, 1982, even up to June 1983, we were starving many times. But since 1983 when we hit the enemy hard, they rarely come through here, and when they do it's quickly and defensively. So we have had time to plant and reap many crops of beans and corn.

I asked about a US invasion.

We are preparing ourselves. We don't want an invasion, but if the Marines come we will hit them hard. If the *gringos* come they are going to have to fight these people, people who have been giving their lives, their blood, for years, and although things will get even bloodier, the *gringos* will have to kill every last one of us before they can say that they have won. We have nothing against the American people and we believe that *they* can stop an invasion, only they can stop Reagan's hunger for blood. They have no reason to come here and die defending – nothing actually – this isn't theirs to defend.

After my interview with María I left for Cordoncillo, where my base is. This time I decided to go alone. I've done this route enough times now not to get lost. Right. Everything went well for the first two hours. Then more and more paths appeared where choices had to be made and I finally got lost. I spend so much energy on my 'Zen and the art of walking' that I don't notice much around me. I found a little boy who understood where I wanted to go and he took me straight down the mountain and deposited me at the bottom of another one. I knew that mountain and it wasn't at all the way I wanted to go. Up the mountain I went – four hours to do a two-and-a-half-hour walk.

I'm feeling demoralized, or lonely, or misplaced, or something. Feeling like it's too much working all alone, trying to cover it all. One day the Popular Power, next day the Christians, next the combatants. Also feeling pressure, time passing and what am I getting? Feeling like I'm going for too much and not getting enough. Hell. . .

She sits and combs her hair over and over again. Combs are very important to Salvadorans. They hang them around their necks, stuff them in their bras, tie them to their belts. I keep losing mine so I use my fingers. Not very Salvadoran of me. But then neither is my body. I'm one of the thinnest women in this part of the world. Most Salvadoran women are rather round, especially in their stomach. When I first arrived at *Propa* I asked one of the plumpest young women how many months pregnant she was. Hum, I'll never ask that again.

Twelve bombs fell around us this afternoon! There I was taking my bath when two A-37s came. Everybody went running off to the bomb shelter or the trench on the other side of the path. I kept on bathing – these planes come all the time, so why should I run? Then the bombs began to fall. I finished my bath, put on my clothes and thought, do I grab my equipment and film and go to the trench or do I stay? Then a bomb fell quite close, the earth trembled and I went to the trench.

We watched as the planes zoomed down, dropped a bomb, then up, then down again. Horacio was just in front and I grabbed his shoulders thinking, this is happening right here, not over there, but right here. It was frightening. After it was over I felt rage, something about jet bombers dumping 500-pound bombs on peasants seemed very cowardly, stupid and wrong.

It's a sad day. I'm very depressed. Two people were killed yesterday in the bombing.

Our people don't have schools, our people lack the basic elements for living, our women still give birth in the hills, our children die in the streets at three months of age. Is this just? Our peasants don't have land, our workers die of hunger because their salary is so low, our people don't have houses, they don't have the right to anything. We are fighting so that our people can have the conditions under which they can develop and create a better life for themselves. And this is what liberty is. Liberty isn't running around wherever you want, catching a plane whenever and for wherever. Liberty is the right to life, to work, to have land, to have schools, to have health, to have art and culture. Liberty is the right to live with dignity. That is why we are fighting, for the right to liberty (excerpt from my interview with Cmte. Douglas).

Twenty-six mortars just fell around us. Keeps the place hopping.

War story: A group of *compas* have been under heavy mortar attacks off and on for days. One night they finally get out of the area and go over to another mountain. In the morning they wake up and find that they are in a lovely place. As they stand admiring the view they suddenly hear a 'whoosh'. They drop to the ground but there is no explosion. This happens four times and the *compas* are beginning to feel ridiculous. Finally they discover what made the noises: the *sopes* (large vultures). It was the air pushing against their wings when they lowered their altitude that sounded like the 'whoosh' of a mortar. Then they really felt ridiculous.

I can't tell if it's thunder or bombs. Gee, what a dilemma. Damn the rainy season. I didn't want to be here for it (beginning of May). But here I am. Next month is going to be difficult living with a battalion and in the rain.

Esteban came by for a quick visit. I told him, jokingly, that I couldn't tell the difference between thunder and bombs. He laughed and said, 'Do you know how you can tell? When it's thunder everyone keeps sitting, when it's bombs they start running.' Then there was a closer boom and he said, 'OK, now we run.'

We are all drinking hot milk. Someone found some powdered milk in a tree and so we're drinking it. Very nice. Also we have real tortillas today – white ones made of corn – not the greenish-brown ones made of *maizillo* (sorghum) that look and taste terrible. The corn from last year's harvest has been consumed and sorghum is a lot cheaper. It is sold as animal feed and only the very poor and the guerrillas eat it. It has half the nutritional value of corn, but the stalks give more than one ear, and when cut down it sprouts itself; it grows anywhere without fertilizer, and when the government forces sweep through they don't bother to destroy it. It is definitely a war food.

There is a new woman here at *Propa*, although not new to the front. Her name is Eva, she's 24 years old with an attractive personality and a great laugh. She told me that she had been in Guazapa with Marianela in March 1983 when they were ambushed by the government forces and Marianela was killed. (Marianela was the president of the human rights organization linked to the Archdiocese of San Salvador. She was in Guazapa documenting human rights violations, which was her job, when the ambush occurred.)

They were with a group of 120 civilians. Twenty-nine were killed and the rest escaped. Eva was shot in the foot and had to crawl on her hands and knees for ten days until she found medical help. During that time she also got her period and so blood all over. A couple of days after she was shot she took off her boot and saw worms crawling inside the wound. The stench from her foot was so unbearable that she wrapped it in plastic to cut down the smell.

Good God! To see worms crawling inside your own body must be horrifying. Her foot is not bad when you think what happened to it. It still leaks some liquid and has to be cleaned and bandaged twice a day. But she can walk although not for long periods. And she laughs and jokes and is quite the life of the group here.

Radio Farabundo reported that in one small town 27 500-pound bombs were dropped, destroying the place. In El Copiñol, 50 peasants – of whom 18 were under 15 years of age – were quartered and then thrown into a hole. In El Roble 23 peasants – ranging from five days old to 73 years old – were killed then covered in acid and burned. According to the Archdiocese's human rights organization 1,954 people have been killed in the first three months of 1984. The killing continues and so do the dollars.

It's Holy Week. Rutilo begins his daily sermons this week on the Radio Farabundo with 'Every day is Holy Week in El Salvador, our people are waiting for the resurrection, for a free world.' I am off to photograph a mass in Jicarito, a little town up on a mountain – where else?

On my way there my guide told me that he had an uncle in Cabañas (another state), a delegate of the word (a lay priest and considered to be subversive by the Salvadoran military), who was picked up by the *Mano Blanca* (deathsquad) four years ago and chopped into bits in a public square. First his hands and arms, then his feet and legs, then his eyes, ears and tongue. They left him there, just a torso, still alive, as an example to other 'subversives'. My guide told the story in a very matter-of-fact voice. I suppose after so much violence it does become matter-of-fact – how else does one live with it?

I didn't like the mass. The people who partook in it, mostly women, were very passive. The delegates mixed in a revolutionary vocabulary but it was forced, did not connect with the people. The words fell to the ground, the people stared at the ground – there was no spirit.

According to what I've read, the Christians in the 1970s were a major force in federations, organizations, mobilizing people, etc. But now I don't know. When I asked Tilo (short for Rutilo) where the Christians were in the war he said, 'Where are they? Everywhere! They are cooks, nurses, combatants, farmers, *comandantes*.' I suppose it's true. In a prolonged war there are other priorities.

I've been thinking about violence again. How to show/document violence? How to describe a people living in an environment of constant violence? And they don't moan about it or cry about it – it just is. It's their history.

How does one express this to the American people? Even though Americans live in a violent society themselves and watch violence on television almost on a daily basis. I don't know.

I have a friend who is a minister working at the National Council of Churches in New York. He told me that last year he was mugged, for the first time, while standing in a phone booth on the Upper West Side. The mugger had a gun and asked for his money while he was talking to his wife. He said it took him over two weeks to get over the rage he felt at having someone point a gun at him. The money didn't matter, it was the gun.

What would he have felt if going to the parking lot in his building he discovered his pregnant wife, naked, womb cut open and breasts cut off, lying on the hood of the car, because he had met with a group of people to read the Bible?

Walking, walking, walking. When I think I've gotten used to it then I go for another walk. How the hell can someone get used to this? As they say here: 'What goes down in Chalate must go up.'

I am at the *escuelita* (military school), hanging around with the *mara*: Salvatierra, Negro Dulce, Nico, Lito and others. Maybe tomorrow I can get some work down. In time, Taina, in Chalateco time.

This school gets a minimum of 50 new recruits per month. Of the 50 about 35 will be combatants and the others will go into different areas such as first aid, logistics, etc. For one combatant you need four others to make that combatant's life possible – cooking, clothing, medical assistance, bringing in materiel, etc.

I photographed some new recruits. They get a minimum introduction to military form and discipline. They learn to take apart, clean and load a gun. The real training will happen in direct action. I also photographed heads of platoons, not in the major battalions but in the ones here in Chalate, getting extra training in camouflage and ambush techniques. The military instructors are old-time combatants who because of injuries cannot keep up with the battalions.

There is an old man here working at the school. He remembers, at the beginning of the war, how nobody believed that they could possibly create their own army, that they could ever have weapons. 'How could we if all the weapons were in the hands of the enemy? How could we take them? Now, look', he said smiling, 'our people are armed, we have an army and we have conquered our own territory.'

I'm staying with the *mara* of instructors and lying in my hammock, everything is tranquil and the birds are tweeting loudly. A *compa* passes by and hands me two small tomatoes. Such gifts. This is a land of extremes; it is tranquil or it is blowing up, one walks like hell or one sits forever, one laughs or cries, lives or dies.

Last night we had one little candle burning and a *compa* from the school came by and asked Salvatierra if he had any candles because they needed light for a special job. Salvatierra responded, 'I have no light but I have the word, many words, actually.' I don't think that *compa* understood but the rest of us roared with laughter.

It reminded me of the first time I met Negro Dulce on my trek across the country. He was leading a column of guerrillas that Guillermo and I joined to get from one place to another. We stopped to rest and Negro Dulce passed around a hunk of sugarcane candy. When we each received our piece he said, 'OK, now that we've eaten the wafer let's go.'

I left the school and am back in Cordoncillo. I was taken half of the way to where I knew the territory and went the rest of the way by myself. On the way I met an old peasant and we walked together. Suddenly two A-37s appeared and began to bomb. Since there wasn't any vegetation we crouched by the side of the mountain and watched. When it was over, the man looked at me and said, 'Those planes with those bombs are the US version of the deathsquads.' I'm beginning to feel like he does because those bombs don't fall on FMLN military camps, guerrillas don't stand in a large group in the open waiting for bombs to fall on them. No. Those bombs fall on civilian houses, are directed against the civilian population.

I went with Laura, buyer for the logistics battalion, to La Laguna, a medium-sized town where the *compas* do a lot of buying. And we went in a truck! A bright red Toyota truck. The *compas* here have *requisado* (requisitioned, a word much used by the guerrillas to describe taking weapons, uniforms, ammo, vehicles, cattle, etc., that belong to the 'enemy') three jeeps and this red truck.

We averaged about ten miles an hour on a road very much like the one I walked on to go to Zapotal. The driver, a large and jovial man with several gold teeth that sparkled when he laughed, said that he'd been in this front for one year. He used to drive a Cherokee for a rich man in San Salvador. When the *compas* were trying to recruit him, since people who know how to drive are hard to find, he said, 'What? The guerrillas drive in cars? You've got to be kidding!' As we bumped along the road he said, 'When I got here I said "you call this a road? This ain't no road, it's a dry riverbed!"'

At one point a bus came in the opposite direction. The two drivers stopped and Manuel, our driver, said he had a tire to be fixed. The bad one was exchanged for a good one from the top of the bus and we drove on. The *compas* seem to have collaborators in many places.

A couple of hours later we arrived in La Laguna: a town with electricity and paved roads. There were a number of *compas* waiting for us, some of whom worked with Laura and others kept track of any 'enemy' movement. I ran around with Laura as she bought boots, clothing, salt, sugar, etc. The stores were typical rural Latin stores selling a little of everything: clothes, food, costume jewelry, pencils, etc. Most of the people in town did not want to have their pictures taken. Part of the town is pro-government, another is pro-FMLN, but some of those do not want to show it openly because of the *orejas* (ears, meaning spies) and because the government forces come through here at times, and the people are scared of being turned in. The National Guard had a post here but they were kicked out a year ago by the FMLN.

We left after dark, the truck two-thirds full of supplies and people. As we passed through several little towns we picked up more *compas* laden with more sacks of corn and beans.

It poured last night. Most people got wet because of the holes in the roof. Mud everywhere. Very depressing. The winter (rainy season) has begun. There is fungus growing on my lenses and film. Shit.

Last day of the month and it's been raining since 02:00 hrs. What a bitch! This next month is going to be a bitch: changing war zones and in the rain.

I finally met with Esteban last night at Julio's place. I'm glad that he's responsible for me because he's good to work with. He listens and considers what I ask, and if he says yes, it's yes right away, and if no then it's no. So far he has not said no. But he did want to know why I insisted on going to Felipe Peña (another front near Guazapa). I said that I needed to be closer to the war, with a battalion that was living it non-stop, and the X-21 is a famous battalion and the FPL's oldest.

'I'll send you to a battalion further up north in Chalate.'

'No. I've heard about Felipe and it's what I want and I think it's important to document.'

'It's a much higher risk front.'

'I know.'

He looked at me a while and then said, 'OK, to Felipe you go. But not tomorrow. Tomorrow we're having the First of May celebration in Ojos de Agua which I think you will like. After that I'll prepare your trip to Felipe.'

Both Julio and Francisco have been telling me the hardships I will live through going to Felipe but that's where I want to go. I feel that I need to understand that aspect of the war. Hell, I think I'll go back to New York City. I don't know if I'm ready for this. But I know I have to do it because it's part of the reality here. My risk: US bombs falling on my US head.

The rest of the evening we laughed over war stories. Lucas, Hector, captain of the X-21, Julio, Francisco, Esteban and myself. At times I would catch Esteban watching me, wondering what I was thinking of the stories, but I was laughing as much as the others.

Francisco told a war story: After a battle the *compas* requisitioned a couple of small trucks. A few of them decided, 'Wow! We'll drive the food to the compas!' So they filled the trucks with beans and tortillas and off they went. They didn't know how to drive but they were like kids with a new toy, and they raced each other and were having a great time, until one of them went out of control and crashed. Francisco was called over to take care of the injured. One *compa*, lying on the ground cried out, 'Francisco, Francisco, I'm terribly hurt, my brains are coming out of my head!' Francisco looked at him and said, 'Those aren't brains, they're beans.' The *compa* wiped his head, looked at them, put them into his mouth, smiled and said, 'Oh wow! Beans!' and proceeded to eat all he could.

We laughed and laughed. They're all such kids. Each story was told with the maximum of drama. It's what I like about their stories: they are not about macho, full-of-bravado Rambos; they're of weaknesses, errors, humor and valor, all mixed up.

Before we broke up for the evening Esteban took me aside and said that while I was at Felipe they would work on a plan to get me out of the country. I can't use my own passport because I was given only ten days to stay in El Salvador. I assume they know what they're doing – I'm not the first journalist to spend time with the FMLN. I really have to believe in them and that they will come up with something so I can get out of here without having my film confiscated, or worse, my life.

May

During the month of April, according to the Farabundo radio, the FMLN destroyed the equivalent of a battalion: they inflicted 357 casualties, took 27 prisoners and captured 119 weapons.

The people at *Propa*, in back of my tree-office, continue to yak away. They go on and on complaining constantly of being tired or sick. Maribel talks non-stop, or complains that her bones hurt, or turns the handle of the mimeograph machine, or looks at herself in the mirror she keeps tucked inside her bosom. I don't know. . . What do I want?

I asked Francisco about the bones hurting. I've never been in a place where people complain about their bones hurting. He said it's because of malaria. If you get malaria often enough, which many do, your joints begin to hurt. I also asked him about my period: two months without it. He said not to worry, that a lot of women, especially the ones who come from the city, don't get their period the first two or three months after they arrive in the front. I should be getting it soon. Oh, well, why should I want it anyway?

Felipe Peña, where I am going, is another front near the Guazapa volcano, covering part of the states of Cabañas and Cuscatlán. It was invaded the day I had wanted to go. There are eight government battalions, airplanes and helicopters all over the place. Everyone is in *guinda*. If it hadn't been for the First of May I would be in that *guinda*. Now I must wait until the invasion is over.

Everything is changing here. *Propa* is moving, Julio and Toño are going elsewhere, Francisco is going out, and I will be going to Felipe. I must pack all the stuff I don't want to take with me and give it to Toño who will take it to the radio for safekeeping.

The Farabundo radio says that the repression in the cities has increased now that the elections are over. There are roadblocks everywhere with soldiers demanding to see the stamped IDs. (Everyone in El Salvador is required to carry an ID at all times. It is a small booklet with all the pertinent information including a photograph of the person. At the back is space for a stamp that proves you voted. If the space is blank the military and police assume you are a subversive and may take you away. To be taken away usually means to be disappeared.) The slogan on the Farabundo, '*tu voto no vale nada*' ('your vote is worth nothing'), should be '*tu voto vale tu vida*' ('your vote is worth you life'). Ninety-four municipalities did not vote; this means, they tell me, that 35 per cent of the country did not vote.

As I sit here I must not forget that this living without repression or fear of the deathsquads and the National Guard is not the norm. That just 15 to 20 kilometers from here, in the larger towns like Chalatenango, and in other major cities and the capital they are ever present.

Esteban came by, all shaved and hair cut. A handsome man. I guess he's going off somewhere. He told me about the chaos and lack of communication during the 1981 offensive. But fight they did and win some they did. Then he described the slow process of creating a unified group under the FMLN. I asked if without the US involvement in the war they could win by the end of the year. He said no, neither militarily nor politically. The FMLN is still not unified, the five groups are still fighting each other politically. But they're working on it. Also the masses need a lot more work. 'No', Esteban said, 'we are not yet ready to take power. But were it not for the *gringos* this war would be ending sooner rather then later.'

Tomorrow I leave for Felipe. What I'm trying not to think about is that I'm going to walk back over a big chunk of the way I first came and then I'm going to do it all over again. The rhythm of the guerrilla: either one sits forever waiting or walks forever going.

I walked six hours with my guide/courier. I thought after two months of conditioning I would get better at this. But no. The opposite. It was worse than when I came from the capital. My pack seemed to weigh more even though I had less in it. Then it poured with rain for several hours. I reached a limit about 40 minutes from the lake and by then it wasn't just the two of us walking, it was a column of *compas* all going to the lake. I stepped out of the column, squatted, stuck my head inside my poncho and pretended I didn't exist anymore. I can't take this anymore, I can't carry the weight, I can't, I can't, I said to myself. A *compa* came by a couple of minutes later, not anyone I knew, and asked me what I was doing there.

'The weight. I can't take the weight anymore.'

'Here, give it to me, I'll take it,' he said in a quiet voice.

After we crossed the lake my guide and I walked another couple of hours. At 23:00 hrs he said, 'OK, you've had enough. Let's find a place to sleep.'

I think it's the food. I can't believe I stepped out of the column and crawled into myself. All the energy was gone. At least when I came into this war I had been eating well before. But after two months of beans and tortillas. How the hell do they do it?

I'm sitting at the command post of Felipe Peña, hidden under dense foliage by the side of a river, waiting for someone to take me to the X-21 battalion. My shirt ripped in several places down my back during the walk so I went to the kitchen and asked if anyone had a needle and thread. One cook said yes but that she only had black thread. I said I didn't care what color it was as long as it kept my shirt – a blue work shirt – on my back. I proceeded to sew using huge stitches. They stared at my agile fingers. Listen ladies, I really don't care what it looks like as long as it covers me. They probably thought I should throw it out but it's the only shirt I have here so it will have to do. Everything will have to do here including me.

The planes really fly around here. Much more than up in Chalate. I can't tell what they are dropping but I can hear machine guns.

Now I'm sitting in a little town called Cinquera waiting for another guide. In the beginning of 1983 this town was attacked by the FMLN, bombed by the Salvadoran military and deserted by the people. About 4,000 people used to live here. It's a pretty place only there is no one here.

Cinquera was a bastion of the National Guard who were notorious for their cruelty and repression. When the FMLN decided to take the town the population was very sceptical: they didn't think anyone could successfully attack the National Guard, especially the FMLN. After the battle the FMLN handed over their National Guard prisoners to the people. The people slaughtered them with machetes.

My combatant/guide came and off we went. It was not a bad walk. We arrived at an abandoned house where a group of *compas* were hanging out under some trees. My guide went over to one of them, saluted and said, '*Compañero*, I have brought you the *gringa*.' We all laughed. I went over to the one being saluted and introduced myself. He was *comandante* Gustavo, head of the battalion. He smiled and said welcome.

We are about 12 kilometers, in a straight line, from the Guazapa volcano and about 26 kilometers from San Salvador. A whole battalion right under the enemy's nose. They showed me the path to the river and I went down to bathe. There was no one around and I bathed all by myself – right under the enemy's nose. I'm getting quite nonchalant about all this.

Gustavo's group is a pleasure to be with. They don't bum things off of you and everything is shared. Very different from other camps I've been in.

I spent the morning talking to the head of provisions and supplies. A battalion consumes 700 pounds of *maizillo* per day – they also have a shortage of corn. Over 50 per cent of the *maizillo*, corn and beans consumed comes from the masses. The rest they have to buy. Also they buy salt, sugar, soap, rice, etc. in the towns. The majority of the people help to feed the troops, not only in the controlled zones but also in the zones of expansion.

There seem to be three types of zones in El Salvador from a FMLN perspective: controlled zones, zones in dispute, which are deserted areas and towns where the government forces and the FMLN come and go, and zones of expansion, which are controlled militarily by the government forces but where the FMLN is expanding its base and support clandestinely.

Even though the FMLN troops requisition uniforms from the government soldiers and barracks they attack, they still need to buy clothing and boots. Most of these supplies come in trucks from San Salvador and are dropped off in clandestine places.

Boots are always a problem because the combatants go through them so fast. The majority wear little black boots; one brand is made in El Salvador and the other in Honduras, and both are available throughout the country. But they don't last long. In the summer they last around two months maximum, in the winter (rainy season) they may last ten to fourteen days. The jungle boots they take from the soldiers last four to five months.

Speaking of boots, I am getting rather tired of talking about mine. They are the main point of interest whenever a *compa* meets me for the first time. He/she looks closely at them, touches them and I tell all about their redeeming features. I am a walking ad for Fabiano boots. I agree, they are indeed a fine pair of boots and I would not have lasted so far without them. They are strong, give complete protection, are waterproof yet allow your feet to breathe, they are dynamite and I can understand everybody wanting a pair. They are much superior to jungle boots. They also cost a lot more. I'm lucky, I admit it.

In the afternoon I spoke with Alicia, head of First Aid and Health. The majority of the first aid nurses are very young women, who know nothing about what they're doing in the beginning. It is a hard post to fill because these young girls are afraid of battles, don't like moving around all the time (which is what a battalion does) and their casualty rates are high. Alicia said that in some combats they've had six to seven nurses killed.

She explained the different posts. First Post is in the line of fire. There is one nurse per company and she carries a knapsack with tape, gauze, band-aids, cotton, alcohol, syringes and pain killers – both oral and injections. This nurse usually knows very little but she is there for immediate first aid. If the *compa* is badly injured he/she is sent to the Second Post.

Second Post is close to the line of fire. It is made up of three nurses who are a little more knowledgeable. They carry the same as the First Post but more of it. They also carry splints, hammocks and serum. Sometimes these three will have to care for 15 *compas* at once.

Third Post is where the very badly injured are taken. It is still with the troops but further from the line of fire. This is a mobile hospital. There are one to two doctors and several nurses. They carry double the supplies of the Second Post plus a number of surgical instruments and perform operations in the field.

Common injuries are bullet wounds in arms and legs. More special ones are in the head, thorax and abdomen. Because of the way the guerrillas live and the food they eat even a small injury can make the person very weak.

When the battle is over the troops go and rest, but not the nurses. They have to take care of the injured. It's a tough life, Alicia said. The patients are ill-humored because they want to be with their buddies and be able to fight. Their friends go off and they have to stay behind. It's the same with those who lose their limbs, she said – they always want to go back and fight.

I asked Alicia how she kept her own spirits up.

'I am very clear about what I am doing and so I have a lot of hope. It's a hard life but I know that what we're fighting for is right.'

'What is that, Alicia?'

'We're fighting so that we can live in our country without being treated like beasts of burden, so that we can live without fear.'

She is 17 years old and has been with the guerrillas for four years. Seventeen. They're all so young. It's incredible. This is an army of kids fighting against a US trained, financed and advised army.

We had a piece of fried fish and a tortilla yesterday. Today we got a chunk of beef, a tortilla and an avocado. As Julio said, eating with a battalion can be nothing, can be a tortilla, can be a quarter of a chicken three times a day. It all depends on where they are and which large landowner is going to have to pay his dues.

I really like Gustavo's group. There are four radio people, a young messenger, and four others that I'm not sure what they do. Patti, one of the radio people, is like their mother. She's 19 years old. She divides all the food. The command post doesn't have a kitchen so our food, when available, is delivered to us and Patti hands it out very equally.

I have found a family nearby who make bread. Neat! This morning I went over to buy some. They were very nice and I ended up staying two hours talking. They gave me fried fish, an avocado, bread and tortillas for breakfast. I felt uncomfortable taking their food, everybody is so poor, but they wanted to share it so I accepted. It was wonderful!

They told me that they come from over there (I'm not sure where that is) then they had to leave. They spent two years in another place and then had to leave. They have been at this base, called Tenango, a year. Last year there were *guindas* almost every eight days. When the enemy left they would come back. Everything would be destroyed, the houses and the crops. The soldiers would even take the time to go up on the roofs to break the tiles. Then they would throw out propaganda from the planes saying, 'Return! Return to your homes!' But a *guinda* every week?

The husband told me that he was listening to the radio last night and Duarte[13] was talking about democracy and all the good things he was going to do for the people of El Salvador. 'But the people don't forget', the husband said, 'He can't deceive us. We know, we remember the two years he was in power before and all the repression and killing and deathsquads. We remember.'

Now that the battalion is hanging around a civilian base it's interesting how many combatants spend as much time as possible with a family. I noticed this in the bases in Chalate. Since most don't have a family anymore they visit families when they are on leave or camped nearby. They hang around, play with the kids, and the wife tries to cook something special for them. I remember when I went to my little store in Chalate I'd find a couple of compas sitting around, their military gear hanging from the beams and trees and then a couple of days later they would be gone. Here too. Even I am being adopted, temporarily, by this family that makes bread.

It's been raining every day but the sun comes out after. The *compas* have fixed the roof of the front porch of the house we are staying in. The major part of the house is in pieces. At night it is quite cozy. Actually for them since I am the only one in a hammock. They throw down their plastics, all in a row, and cuddle up in their sheets, giggling and telling stories. Even Gustavo. He's always in the middle of them. Last night he yelled out, 'Hey, Taina, if you get lonely up there you can come down here with the proletariat!'

'Thanks, Gustavo, but the problem is not class, the problem is the bones on the ground.'

'The problem is that you don't eat enough. You never eat your ration of tortillas,' Patti yelled back.

Eventually we all quieted down and Patti made the nightwatch list. The length of time each person does depends on how many are sleeping there.

Interview with Jacobo, a 26-year old peasant from Chalatenango:

At 18 he was drafted by the government military. Every Sunday he would listen, on his little radio, to Monsignor Romero's sermons. After a demonstration in February 1977, in which many people were killed, Romero gave a moving sermon that touched him deeply and he decided to desert. He went to see a cousin who was 'organized' (meaning in the opposition) and said he wanted to join. His first job was to work with peasants, helping them organize their demands for higher wages and more food while they labored in the fields. The government's response to those demands was 'kill them'. Many people he knew had their heads broken open by machetes. He then decided that organizing was worthless and asked to be incorporated into the armed fight.

He joined a clandestine guerrilla group at the end of 1979. They used wooden rifles in their basic training because there were few weapons and none could be used just for training.

His first fight was very frightening. Twelve of them, armed with a couple of pistols and one carbine, were ordered to destroy a small patrol of nine soldiers and to requisition ten cows. They killed a couple of cows in the chaos but they succeeded. From that fight they got a couple of G-3s, and so they were better armed and feeling slightly more courageous for the next one.

In the beginning the only thing that gave them courage, that kept their morale up, was the hatred for the government forces, especially the National Guard. The only capable and evil fighters, according to Jacobo, are the National Guard and the Atlacatl (the most elite battalion in the Salvadoran military). 'The rest', he said, 'don't amount to much. You talk to them after a couple of rounds, yell over for them to give themselves up and they usually do. Plus they are not evil. They've just been forced to fight and so they do but without much energy or belief.'

In the early days the National Guard used to make fun of the guerrillas. During one fight, Jacobo had an M-1 (the National Guard use G-3s – bigger caliber bullets and lethal) and a National Guard yelled out to him, 'OK kid, you can stop throwing *maizillo* at me!' (Sorghum grows in little round pellets.) Jacobo took out a homemade contact bomb and throwing it yelled, 'There's my *maizillo*!'

I've seen and heard on military radios, American advisors directing the government troops in battle. They accuse us of having advisors. I've never seen the Cubans, Nicaraguans and Russians they say are here. And you know what? We resent that accusation. Even the masses get angry when they hear that because they know that what we have today was done by us, our work, our lives, this is ours. And you know, in the beginning the people didn't believe we could do it. But now they've seen what we've done, they've seen our victories. And who are we fighting? Against men that the people like? The National Guard, the government forces, the deathsquads? The people are tired of this war. Who isn't? But they won't and we won't give up now.

It's a sultry day. I went down to the river to bathe. It's crazy, by the time I climb back up to camp I'm covered in sweat but it's sweat bathing a clean body. Lots of planes going by, lots of bombs falling over there. As far as I'm concerned, when it comes to bombs and mortars, if they're not falling on you they're falling over there.

Last night Gustavo went off to a meeting and stayed the night. As I was snuggled in my hammock a hand shook me and said, '*Compa, compa*, it's time for the nightwatch.' It was the twelve-year old. The order of the watch is from the beginning of the row of sleeping bodies to the end. He was at the end and decided I was next. I said OK. I wasn't about to wake anybody. I got out of my hammock and he handed me an M-16. I slung it over my shoulder and walked away from the house, sat on a rock and lit a cigarette. This is crazy, I thought to myself, I don't even know how to use an M-16, and here I am, a *gringa*, doing nightwatch for the command post of the X-21! Good God! If the enemy comes, what do I do? I'm responsible for all these bodies tucked inside their sheets. I knew that I really wasn't, that the command post was surrounded by a battalion and I wasn't protecting anyone. But still. I was amused and also taken aback with the idea that here I was in the hour just before dawn with an M-16 on my shoulder, watching for what?

Interview with Alberto, an 18-year old former bricklayer:

Last year in July he was going home from work when the National Guard arrived in his town and surrounded several blocks and picked up all of the young men, including himself, and took them off to a barracks in another town. From there they were shipped to Honduras for military training. Most of the trainers were *gringos*. After a month and a half, they were sent back to El Salvador. At the barracks they were often told that the guerrillas were 'black, bearded, ugly Cubans and when they capture you they tear your skin off piece by piece.'

Even so, during his first major battle, last November, he and nine others surrendered. (In 1982 the FMLN decided that any soldier who surrendered would not be killed. A big propaganda campaign went out informing the soldiers 'surrender and your life will be respected.') The *compas* stripped them of their uniforms, boots and weapons, and gave them old clothing in replacement. They were taken to a camp and after a week they were individually asked if they wanted to stay or go back. He and four others decided to stay.

'Why?' I asked.

'Because if you're just a soldier, without any rank, in the government army, you're treated like a dog. But here the *comandantes* and anybody else with rank dress the same way you do, eat the same food, live the same way. Everybody is equal and friendly and they know why they are fighting and it's sort of like a family. So I decided to stay.'

We had a quarter of a chicken apiece today for lunch and for dinner, nothing. Not even a *tortilla*. Tomorrow we move.

It was a nice walk. Only three hours and all rolling hills. I like this area of El Salvador. We've set up base in another blown-up house. Patti is killing bats and I'm talking to David, who has just arrived and will be staying a while.

David's been with the FPL for eight years, doing a variety of things. Now, I think, he is some kind of political coordinator, visiting all the fronts throughout the country. I say, I think, because many times, within the FMLN, you don't know exactly what someone does and it's not correct to ask. I suppose it has to do with any guerrilla structure where knowledge means betrayal if you are picked up by the enemy.

He's in his early thirties and used to be a farmer. Farming is the love of his life. Two years ago he was walking with his two children and nine other people when they were ambushed by the government forces. Seven were killed, including his children. His wife, also with the FPL, is now pregnant and 'we are going to start again', he said with a gentle smile.

Gustavo has told me that during the time I am scheduled to be here they don't have any major battles planned. Anything else he can help to arrange he will gladly do, but not a battle. Next month, yes, some interesting things are going to happen, but this month is going to be rather quiet. Damn!

This morning while we were walking from there to here Gustavo said that a company of the battalion was going on a little job. It would be a three-day walk. Did I want to go?

'Three-day walk?'

'Yes, three going and three coming back – they can only move in complete darkness.'

'Is it going to be interesting?'

'In terms of photography I don't know. It will happen at night, very quickly, and then back again.'

'Oh God, I'm not going to walk six nights to shoot in the dark. But thanks for the invitation.'

This afternoon while I was sitting with David, Gustavo came up and told us to be ready to go with him at 14:00 hrs. 'We're going to say goodbye to the troops.'

On the way, Gustavo, who is also of peasant origin and loves to farm, talked about farming with David. Here I am with the *comandante* of the famous X-21 and David, on our way to say good luck to the troops, and they're talking about farming.

We arrived at an area filled with trees. I saw a large group of kids sitting around on the ground. Some were resting, others were goofing off and laughing. Then some guys came with a big bag of bullets and another with tortillas and handed them out: 100 bullets and three tortillas per combatant. Two things struck me: one was seeing tortillas lying on the grass next to bullets and M-16s, and the other was their age. I've met combatants off and on here and there and everywhere, but I've never seen a big group of the them all together. They're just kids, and they act like kids, except that most have uniforms, all have M-16s and they are about to go off to battle.

Time to get into formation. Off they went into an open field. I counted approximately 100 kids. The sun was going down through some clouds, the Guazapa volcano was in the background on the left, and Gustavo was facing them. They were quite a sight: all sizes, shapes, girls, boys, most had M-16s, some had M-60s, others grenade launchers, and others with extra knapsacks packed with homemade grenades and explosives, and all very serious. All the laughing and joking were over. These were guerrillas.

Gustavo told them, without naming the place, what they were going to do. He said that unfortunately many *compas* were wearing boots that were falling apart, that ammunition was low, that their numbers were few, but that's the way it was at the moment. Therefore, they should think in pure guerrilla tactics which meant acting creatively with what the situation demanded. They were going into a territory they didn't know and here were their two guides who knew the territory well and to trust them. Good luck, good fighting, some FMLN slogans and they filed quietly off into the dark. Those kids that had been children just minutes ago were now adults going off to war and some of them might get killed.

I'm beginning to get a sense of all this. I'm beginning to understand how difficult it must have been for many to believe that they, the guerrillas, would be where they are today: their own army, their own territory where you can walk day or night from Chalate to Guazapa (just to name these two fronts). 'All the old-timers, all the organizers, they didn't get to see what we accomplished,' David said.

I also think that the Salvadoran people themselves, outside of the guerrilla, must feel a certain pride not only because it is their sons and daughters, the *muchachos* and *muchachas*, who have accomplished this, but because of who the guerrillas are fighting, as Jacobo said. If nothing else, the odds are more even now, which means that the National Guard, the deathsquads and the military can no longer attack with impunity, as they did throughout the 1970s.

We moved again this morning. About a four-hour walk and I didn't mind it at all. Maybe it's because I'm with a group I enjoy being with, and these are hills and not mountains. We talk and stop when we find mangos. Only my feet, as usual, hurt like hell. Like hell I would like to add.

War story: The *compas* were cleaning up after a major battle, picking up an assortment of weapons, etc. As they approached what had been the enemy command post, they saw a new box on the ground. Everyone eyed it but didn't go near it. Finally a *compa* picked it up ever so gently and carried it over to their command post. Everybody there looked at it nervously until a bomb specialist came, walked around it, sniffed it, and then slowly opened it. Inside was a nightscope for an M-16.

There is only one reality: war. That's all these kids talk about, it's all they know. And what else is there? There's no book store down the mountain, and anyway most of them can't read, there aren't any movie theaters or televisions. This is it, this is their world, and it's full of teenagers. And they're very much like teenagers anywhere else, except that their school is war, their friends are combatants and they are peasants. They love rock and roll, they love to dance and they have their own way of dancing with their M-16s slung, casually, over their shoulders. (I've been to dances that were so packed that the banging of M-16s against each other was louder than the music. I would think they'd want to get rid of the gun to dance but, no, not the guerrillas. They wear their best uniforms and their harness and gun – which can weigh over ten pounds – and that's the way they like to dance.) They have their own slang and their own style, within the limitations – it's the rolling up of the sleeves, the pants that are taken in so that they fit snug around the hips. They're kids, teenagers. And instead of talking about the things that teenagers talk about in the US, they talk about war.

Only I get bored talking about war. OK, so I don't have my own war stories to tell, but how many times can you tell a story? If they don't talk about war they sing along with the radio. Their favorites are American rock and roll songs. They imitate the English sounds without having any idea of what they are saying, and sing right along. It's very funny. Many times I've been asked, both here and in Chalate, to translate a song. Now the number one hit song with the guerrillas is Stevie Wonder's 'I Just Called to Say I Love You'. I don't know how many times I've translated that one. It's very strange to be walking through the mountains and hear 'I just called. . .' blaring through the air. I shall forever associate Stevie Wonder's song with these mountains and kids.

They've just killed a cow a few yards from where I'm sitting. Poor thing. Its calf is standing next to her. How sad. Oh, well, it's protein for a battalion. Two days worth of food? Less? They're taking the calf away but it doesn't want to leave its mother. Oh dear. I will probably eat it. It's called fresh meat.

The 'explorer'(O-2A spotter plane) is flying around dropping rockets here and there. Now it's coming back. Hard to cover a cow. Here it comes again. We must be just a few air minutes from the capital. This country is just too small for comprehension. If the Vietnamese thought their country was small, what would they think this was?

Here comes an A-37. I wonder if they can see the cow? Boom! One down. . . two. . . now three. . . four further away (I don't think they know what they are doing). . . five and over. There are dozens of vultures circling over the dead cow, or what is left of it. If the pilot were smart he would bomb right around here. Fortunately the pilot is not smart – not yet. The buzzards have gone. Bury the carcass, I say. Oh, well, I think I'll go back and sit in my hammock again.

I finally took a bath in a puddle of water at the bend of a river that has not yet reacted to the rainy season. Feel much better.

I did absolutely nothing today, nothing. Sat in my hammock all morning. There was no food. Then at lunch they sent us tortillas and hunks of meat in a broth. I said I didn't want any meat. Patti looked at me wide-eyed and went and got me an avocado she had in her knapsack. Thank you, thank you very much.

The A-37s are here again, so in with our clothes. The scream they emit when they dive, just before they drop the bomb, is unnerving. Well, now that I'm out of my hammock I should go find a place where a bomb won't fall. These are pretty close. Not close enough. Back out with the clothes. Think I'll go sit in my hammock. . .

Dinner came: tortillas, nothing else. Patti opened a big can of meat and started heating it up. It actually looks good but it's probably for the honchos that have been meeting all afternoon with Gustavo, planning tomorrow, the day after and maybe even next year. Think I'll smoke another cigarette.

Well, we had quite a dinner. Canned meat on tortillas, coffee and sweet-bread! If one person eats here, everybody eats here. I would love to know what these guys are planning and how they discuss it.

I shot a class on how to use a grenade launcher and how to move around with it. It looks like I'm not going to get much here. Paco told me that there isn't much happening because most of the companies are off doing something or other – there just isn't anyone around. I guess I need a lot more time in this place to photograph it right. Anyway, it looks like I leave for Chalate tomorrow. This is it.

I'm sitting here in my hammock and once again thinking about wars of liberation, revolutions, or whatever you want to call them. In terms of this one I'm still trying to figure out what makes it click, what makes it sustainable. A couple of thoughts come to mind: the repression and violence used against the majority of these people reached a saturation point – if you are constantly forced up against a wall, eventually you decide to shoot your way out of that position because to remain stationary is to be shot down yourself. So they join the FMLN. Why? There are those who through the political struggles in the 1970s acquired an understanding of the political and economic forces that have shaped their country and they join to change those forces. Others join as a way of fighting state terrorism, either for very personal reasons or because of the overall environment such a state creates. Some join simply because fighting is better than accepting the dull, hard and deadend existence of their peasant parents and grandparents. A few join because that is what their generation is doing.

Being a guerrilla is having power, power to act, to react to so many years of impotence. Being a guerrilla is their revenge against a system that has directly or indirectly violated their lives. Also, I think that as the war continues (it's gone on for four years now), becoming part of the FMLN represents a way of life, has become a lifestyle: it takes care of them, clothes them, feeds them – is a family – and, most important, the majority are of the same age group. And they must learn something new. Whether illiterate or not, the fact of being with the FMLN, of living this way, teaches them more than they would be learning tucked away on some miserable rocky piece of land. No?

Anyway, I think that this type of war is made possible, livable and fightable because of their history. A history of repression, violence and poverty. These are the reasons for this war.

Well, I can see that getting out of any place is always going to be difficult. I can't leave today because there is enemy activity up in Chalate.

Cesar invited me to a class for a section of a company. He talked about national, international and military affairs, about the FMLN and the FPL. That they have accomplished great battles but must keep up the momentum. He emphasized that they must be very clear about why they are fighting; that machismo, or that the enemy killed your father or sister or blew up your house, were not the right reasons. That aside from the problems with clothing, food and ammunition, the other major problem was dysentery. 'This is your own fault, we have built outhouses and nobody uses them. When the rain comes, the shit washes down to the rivers and then we drink from the rivers.'

The combatants were not that interested, as is the case with most teenagers when you put them in a class. Most of these kids are simple folk, so what do they care about international maneuvers or about shitting in a hole? They've been shitting wherever they please all of their lives – why should they change? I am not being sarcastic. I am trying to understand and look at things as they are.

However, I do think that the slogan '*Viva el partido Marxista-Leninista*' ('Hurrah for the Marxist-Leninist party') repeated every time after formation, and on other occasions, is absurd, if for no other reason than that these kids have no idea what the hell it means. Nor do they have any idea of what they're singing when they sing the 'Internationale'. I mean what do those words mean to peasant guerrillas? I think they should invent their own song, with words that connect with the kids, that makes them feel proud or whatever, but some kind of emotion.

I had a talk with Gustavo. He has an incredible brain going a mile a second and his words can't keep up. The guy is sharp, very sharp. He's 26 years old and became organized at 16. He comes from a peasant family and knows how to grow just about everything, plus raise cattle. He worked as a day laborer in sugarcane, coffee and cotton. Around that time he began to look around at his world and think about it. He taught himself to read and write. He entered this area in 1981 and went the whole route: worked with the masses, organizing them, creating bases, planned cooperatives, built houses; then he went into the militias, then into the guerrilla columns (these were the first armed groups, then as they grew they created the UV – *unidades de vanguardia* – then the battalions and the brigades) and now he is a *comandante* of a battalion.

He spoke a lot about strategy and so fast that I didn't get it all. With each new FMLN advance a bigger army is required, and different and more complex strategy. With a bigger army you have bigger problems feeding, clothing and supplying them. There are almost universal laws or strategies for a guerrilla war, but they must be adapted to the national reality. Therefore flexibility and creativity are extremely important.

I asked him about the 'obligatory military service' recently begun by the FMLN. What did this mean? Gustavo does not answer a question directly. He gives you background, sets past events into perspective, etc. What is military history, strategy, tactics? The enemy has had years of studying and the *compas* only four and a half. In these four and a half years the *compas* have succeeded in cutting off the fingers of the hand of those in power. What is left are the major cities and the large landholdings of the oligarchy.

With this increase in FMLN military ability, the US is pouring more money into the war, training more troops and using more sophisticated weaponry. There may even be a US invasion. So the FMLN is entering a new stage in combat. To enter this new stage they need more combatants. How are they going to get them? Voluntary service has worked till now, but it is not enough. One of the reasons it is not enough is that the enemy has succeeded, to a degree, in terrorizing the population, forcing them to leave their homes and go to the capital, or refugee camps within or outside of the country, or getting them into a 'pacification' program. So what the FMLN has begun this year is to go to large towns, hold a public meeting explaining that they are going to take the teenagers and talk to them. At a camp somewhere they explain to the kids that in a country at war there are only two choices to make: fight for the enemy – government forces – or fight against them. Either way they will have to fight. They explain who they are, what they are fighting for, etc. Then they tell them that they can stay or go home. 'A guerrilla war can never be fought or won by people who have been forced to fight. It doesn't work,' Gustavo said.

'There is nothing romantic about this kind of war', Gustavo continued, 'We need to be clear politically and militarily in what we are doing. And we must always act with imagination. Spontaneity and flexibility are what make us strong. We must always be clear that we are fighting for the people and that one, as an individual, must do what is necessary for the whole. Whatever I am asked to do I do and if I fall, others will take my place.'

He ended the conversation with, 'Within all of this we must learn to laugh. We cannot be demoralized. We must laugh.'

Well, I got out of Felipe, but what a walk!

I arrived at Felipe's command post at 11:00 hrs. I was introduced to Rosario and Lili, both with the FPL, who were also waiting to go to Chalate. We were told that a large group was going there and that we could join them.

Finally, at 14:00 hrs a long column of people appeared. We were told they were FAL[14] people going to set up a base in Chalate. There must have been about 70 of them. The column was reorganized and Rosario, Lili and I were placed two-thirds of the way into it. Up ahead, leading the column, was a plump man with long gray hair, wearing a cowboy hat and sitting on a horse. I couldn't believe it, he was sitting on a horse! Looking around me I felt that I was with a large group of hippies getting ready to go off for a walk in the countryside.

The reason I felt this way is that until now the majority of the people I had been with were definitely peasants, either very poorly dressed or in uniforms. This column seemed to be made up of middle-class people, mostly well dressed, many wearing new boots (the brown ones that you can buy in San Salvador) and new knapsacks; a number of them wore glasses and they related to each other in a more sophisticated manner. They did seem to me to be out on a pleasant hike.

This was corroborated in the manner in which they walked. When the column was finally moving, we walked a little, then rested and then walked a little more. This didn't suit me at all, as I knew what lay ahead and I needed to get into my walking mode or I wouldn't make it.

While we were on our third rest in 45 minutes I said to my FPL friends that at this rate we'd never make it to Chalate and that I thought we should find our courier and go on, just the four of us. I finally convinced them and the courier, and off we went. We got to the lake at 17:30 hrs and the *compas* were just getting the boats ready. Where was the FAL group?

We waited until 19:30 hrs and crossed. At the other side, our courier was told that we had to wait for the FAL group because we all had to go together. Damn! We waited. At 01:00 hrs they finally arrived on our side of the lake.

After much ado the column was reorganized. We couldn't use flashlights for the first several hours. It wasn't raining, but the path was deep in mud and covered with rocks. Well, we *inched* our way along the dark mud. Many kept falling up ahead, we were told, and so it was slow. Then the dawn arrived but that didn't seem to make any difference to them. They walked a little, stopped, walked a little and stopped. It was driving me up the wall. My feet were killing me and I knew that at this snail's pace it would only get worse. On top of everything was the fact that we three had not eaten since noon yesterday and these people ate whenever they stopped. They had all kinds of neat things: crackers, cheese, bread, etc. Did they offer us any?

After a while, by the way they were looking around, I said to the FPL *compas*, 'These are a bunch of hippies looking for a scenic spot to have their breakfast!'

'Taina, lower your voice', said Rosario. 'We are working on the unity (between the five groups), remember? Now, be nice.'

At 09:00 hrs we arrived at Los Ranchos. If the three of us and our courier had walked alone we would have been at the Chile (command quarters of the Chalate front) by 09:00 hrs!

I was right. They looked around Los Ranchos, a pretty deserted town with a large white church, and said, 'Yes, this is where we'll have breakfast.'

'Fuck it', I said to Rosario and Lili, 'I will not sit here and watch them eat breakfast. This is ridiculous. We can find our own way from here. We'll get a *compa* to lead us to the beginning of the path and we can go the rest of the way ourselves.'

At first they didn't think it was a good idea to leave the group. But I finally convinced them and off we went at a clippety-clop pace.

My feet were a mess, and worse, I didn't have any fuel left. I have no fat so I can't store any energy, plus what energy was there to store if we hadn't eaten in 18 hours? I was thinking of that huge mountain we would soon have to climb. Then I remembered the little store just before the ascent. I had money so I invited the *compas* to breakfast. We had coffee, beans and tortillas. Lovely! We got to the mountain at 11:00 hrs and up we went.

At the top we split. Lili was going to the Chile and Rosario had to contact so-and-so. I told Rosario to come with me and when we got to *Propa* she could send a message. What I thought was the short-cut proved to be the long way. Poor Rosario! We arrived at *Propa* at 16:00 hrs! Never let Taina be your guide in these mountains, never.

June

Propa has left and a small group of *compas* are staying here in the house. We have decided to call the place the Cordoncillo Parking Lot. One left and came back the same day – couldn't get through to Felipe – another left two days ago and came back yesterday, one left yesterday for who knows how long. Several of us are simply parked long-term, hoping that the fungus won't destroy all the work or the brain, or that this eternal waiting will not obfuscate the reason for being here in the first place.

There is a core of four of us full-time waiters: two Salvadorans, a Mexican and myself. The Salvadorans are waiting to go to different fronts, the Mexican has just entered the front and is waiting to start her teaching project, and I am waiting to be told how and when I can leave this front and this country.

Chevo is head of the parking lot and people come and go either to meet with him, or they are just short-term waiters, waiting for others. It's an interesting crowd with a large turnover. Since there is no kitchen here we take turns going up the mountain to a camp to pick up our ration of beans and *maizillo* tortillas.

House in La Laguna, Chalatenango. Graffiti on the wall says (L to R): 'Young person: before the puppet army recruits you, join the guerrilla of the FMLN.'

Carlitos (ex-combatant and now security for *Propa* due to injuries) with his girlfriend

Elena (from *Propa*) sewing

Horacio (journalist for Radio Farabundo) working on *Propa*'s veranda

Making uniforms in Tamarindo, Chalatenango. Sign on the wall says 'for the spilled blood, onward comrade' and below the sewing machine 'FPL = FMLN = united love and peace'

May 1st celebration in Ojos de Agua, Chalatenango

Father and son
during May 1st
celebration

Negro Dulce
(military
instructor) during
maneuvers

A combatant participating in maneuvers

Military hospital in abandoned adobe house

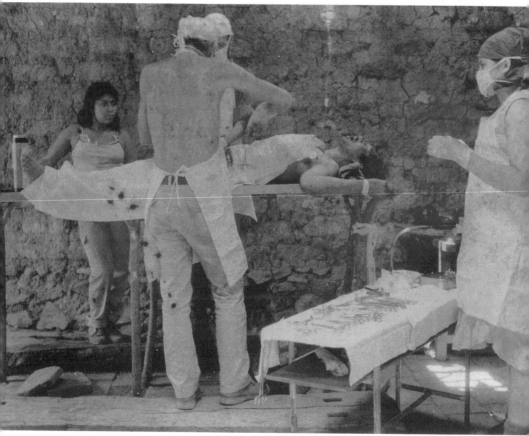

María, sub-regional president of Popular Power in 1984, Chalatenango

Militia voting in municipal elections, Tamarindo, Chalatenango

Some of the local representatives meeting to discuss the government agenda during sub-regional elections, Tamarindo, Chalatenango

Escuelita (military school), Chalatenango

Combatant of the X-21 battalion after the night attack on large chicken farm, Cabañas

Section of the X-21 battalion preparing for battle

Working in the command post of the Felipe Peña Front, Cabañas

X-21 combatant

X-21 combatants getting into formation before going on an attack

One of Gustavo's radio operators

Changing camp with Gustavo's group, Cuscatlán

Local Popular Power president's son, Tamarindo, Chalatenango

Funeral of child killed by mortar during the first day of the August invasion by government forces, Tamarindo, Chalatenango

Remnants of the massacre by government forces during August invasion, Chalatenango

Duarte is talking about a possible dialogue with the FDR-FMLN.[15] If this is a major item on the agenda then I suppose the *compas* will not plan any major offensives or attacks so as to show their willingness to sit down with the 'other side'. Because while I sit here doing nothing I could have stayed with the X-21, but if they are not going to do anything then I would have sat there too. So what difference would it, does it, make? Sit here, sit there, sit anywhere.

Antonio, who works in expansion, is here for a few days. He's very thin and taut. I feel that his nerves vibrate. He spent two years as a FPL urban commando in San Salvador in 1979–81. Then he fought two years with the FES – the FPL's Special Forces. (This is a small battalion made up of the best – they are the commandos of the guerrillas and operate all over the country.) He was badly injured last year resulting in a foot that goes completely numb after walking a short time. Now he works with *Propa* in the area of expansion.

He said that an urban commando or a FES usually works alone or with a very small, tight-knit group. You go on an assignment knowing that you have a 50-50 chance of getting out alive, and that if one in the group falls, probably all will. If soldiers start shooting before your operation is completed, you cannot respond as you would blow the whole game. Often soldiers shoot because they panic easily – it could be just a noise or tension that makes them pull the trigger. Most times they don't even know if anyone is out there, and if someone is, they don't know where. So you hope it's that and don't respond. There is a famous saying by one of the officers of the FES: 'You have to wait until the bullets are closer than just brushing against your skin!' No wonder Antonio is taut.

He told me the latest tactic of the ERP[16] in Morazan: the enemy does a lot of reconnaissance, figures out where he thinks the guerrillas are and sends in an invading force – thousands of soldiers and planes. They move in closer and closer to the 'target' and discover *no one*. Sweating and panting and frustrated they leave. While they were finding no one the guerrillas have mined their retreat. The soldiers turn round and on their way back the land blows up, forcing them to move in columns between the mines. Further down, a small group of guerrillas waits, well hidden, and shoots at the approaching column.

Antonio said that a guerrilla never plays the enemy's game and *always* has, at least, one alternate plan. You must, obviously, have the movability and coordination to implement rapidly any alternative plan. And you *never* use the same plan twice in the same way.

Living in the front becomes quite mundane. Emotions are stabilized – no great feelings until the next *guinda* or combat. As if emotions were stored or spent on those occasions and the day-to-day is kept even – part protection, part reality itself. The world as they know it and live it. Life is simple and you take it as it comes: when there is food, you eat; when there isn't, you don't. Deep passions don't seem to be operative in this war. *Compas* die, are wounded or maimed, new ones come; attachments, relationships, are not developed too deeply. Is this because of class, culture, war? Women continue to have babies, men plant, the kids giggle and time passes. Eva once said, 'Time we have a lot of, life just a little.'

I spend my time listening. That's been and is my job. When I get tired or bored with listening I retire into myself. Throughout these four months, few have asked anything about me. Conversing, as I know it, is not part of the peasant culture – meaning the exchange of ideas and information, the exchange of selves. I've learned a lot but it's been very difficult.

Everybody bunches up at night in that small, dark, flea-covered, bat-filled room. It's the only room that is completely dry. I've strung my hammock in the large room, between two beams where no water falls and I've been all by myself. Now Randu is here and he has strung his hammock next to mine. He's quite a fellow, always with a big grin, ready for anything. Right now he's 'making love': put lots of sugar in a cup, add a little instant coffee then slowly add drops of water while beating it like hell. Half an hour later you have tan fluff. Oh well, another way to eat sugar.

'Pedrito the Duck' came by. He's a famous doctor in these fronts. A couple of years ago the *compas* were taking one of these mountains. They were crawling on their bellies, stopping and going. One *compa*, when he stopped, felt a sharp pain in his stomach. He moved a little and felt other sharp pains. He discovered that he was lying on a nest of vipers. He was taken to Pedrito and Pedrito wondered what to do with him. There was an old peasant helping with the wounded and she said to kill a duck, cut it in half and place it on the bites. Pedrito thought it an old wives' tale, but he had nothing to lose, and there happened to be a duck around. He made some incisions into the bites, killed the duck and put it over them. A couple of days later another doctor came through, and when he passed that *compa* he asked what was the matter with him. Pedrito uncovered him and discovered the rotting duck. 'Oh my God! I forgot the duck!' The kid was alive and without pain. Thus Pedrito became known as 'Pedrito the Duck'.

Pedrito told me that in 1980/81 there were many doctors in the front and others waiting to come. Most of them thought the war would last a couple of months and then there would be an insurrection. Since that didn't happen most of them returned to the cities. So, for a couple of years, over 50 per cent of the doctors were internationalists. Now two-thirds are Salvadorans, and more are coming.

Randu left last night. I feel sad. We had some long conversations in the dark, lying in our hammocks before going to sleep. He always impressed me with his humor, his disposition and his smile. He is 20 years old. He became politicized at age 13 when he was working in a factory and got involved in strikes and demonstrations for higher wages. He has worked fulltime with the FPL for the last five years. He was working in expansion and is now being sent to a battalion. 'Our lives don't belong to us, they belong to the people,' he said.

He was constantly eating and drinking whatever was around. Insatiable. If there were cigarettes, 'Let's smoke them, if not, what the hell.' Let's eat it all today, the hell with tomorrow attitude. Now I feel stupid because I thought we should save some for tomorrow. Felt terrible when he left. To hell with saving anything for tomorrow, it's now that matters, right now, and the future when the war is over. These are the only times: now and then. I promised him my bluejeans when I leave. He was very happy about that.

I've decided to change the name of Parking Lot to the Cordoncillo Hilton and I'm the innkeeper as I'm the only fulltimer left. Tita, the Mexican, came by for a visit. Even though she can talk nonstop she's a very good person. Always ready to do anything, help anyone, and gives and shares all that she has. She is shorter than I am, and plumper, but we both have short hair and the same coloring and our names being somewhat similar, Tita and Taina, people confuse us for each other, that is, people who don't really know us. She's an educator and will be working with the masses in the bases. Until that is worked out by the organization she is here in the hotel, and now is helping at a course that's being given. I assume it's a political/ideological course. She's not permitted to attend, but she helps with the cooking and runs errands. At least she's doing something!

I think the functioning of the organization is quite impressive in terms of the number of people, the different types of people and the variety of areas they work in. But I don't think that time is used well or that some of the people are in the right jobs. I find people very complacent around here. The publications I've seen coming out of *Propa* are very dry and sloganish without feeling or passion that can reach people.

I know that it's not for me to judge and I know there's a lot I don't know what with all of the compartmentalization but. . . I find that a lot of people are lazy and *Propa* was a prime example. And *Propa* is not atypical. I've seen cooks, messengers and many others who just hang around until ordered to do something.

I'm sure it's very difficult to run a war and they can't do everything all of the time. I also know that 1981-83 had a military priority but I think they have to get back to political work or they're going to lose people.

The Farabundo radio also reflects some of these problems. I don't think their approach appeals to peasants or to the working class. I listen to it to get the latest info on enemy activity and combats. But other than that the few other programs they have I don't think are very appealing. It's too dry, too repetitive, too much the 'revolutionary' radio.

Nery and his girlfriend, the cook, down where Julio was staying, deserted day before yesterday. I never saw Nery do much except hang around and then he got pissed off because he wasn't given a new pair of boots, so he deserted, went to Las Mesas refugee camp in Honduras. How does one give spirit and meaning to a person who hangs around all day? I think education should be a priority, but it's not my war and I'm not running it, and they will do things their way. I'm not a peasant and I don't understand how these peasant girls continue to have babies, wear bright yellow or even white dresses (in a war), chit-chat all day long and are perfectly happy to do nothing once the tortillas are made.

I make my coffee, pour it into a cup, sit down with my notebook preparing to write, and boom, bunches of people come, and some go, and some wait. I don't understand why people have to wait so much. They come for a meeting with someone, and three days later they are still here waiting. And they laugh all day. They get wet, boots soaked, fleas biting all night, sleep on hard ground, mud everywhere, wait, go from there to here, from here to there, wait some more, and in the midst of it all they laugh. Incredible.

I just shot some horses laden with cartridges and food. The *compa* taking care of them said, 'You must come from another place. You have a feel for nature, no?'

'What do you mean?'

'Well, you like nature, you have a sense of poetry, no?'

'Well, yes, but what do you mean?'

'Because you are taking photographs of horses. To us a horse is just a beast of burden, so very common. We would never think to photograph them.'

I am saving all of my empty cigarette packs. I start fires with them, use them to send messages, but most important they are perfect toilet paper. One pack is perfect for one shit a day. Learn to use everything here. I lost my pen so Chevo gave me a tiny pencil which I guard with my life and am now writing in my notebook in tiny letters because I don't want to run out of paper.

Chevo is staying here again and he has just given me an almost brand new military shirt. Neat! He said he was tired of seeing me run around in my ragged one. I'm very pleased with it.

He woke up at 05:00 hrs this morning and began to sing at the top of his lungs and he can't carry a tune. Then he came running into my room yelling and banging away trying to kill what he said was a biting *cucaracha*. Right, Chevo. Then he turned on the radio, at full blast, to a Salvadoran Country & Western station. Such violence in the morning! He made coffee and we talked and laughed.

Then Ruth and Tita arrived and I was drawing. Then an A-37 flew by a couple of times and Ruth and Tita went running out to the trench. I kept drawing. A half hour later they came back. Ten minutes later the commercial jet flew over and they ran out again, but they realized what it was and came back. Ruth stopped in front of me, watched me draw for a few seconds and then said, 'You know, Taina, you must be aware of these planes.'

'I hear them, I know which ones they are by the sound they make and I can, usually, tell if they are going to bomb', I said. Fuck off, Ruth, I do not like to be treated like a child, neither will I get hysterical about planes, thank you very much.

I continued to draw. (I am making a humorous drawing of my plight here waiting at the Cordoncillo Hilton.) Then the *compas*, down the hill, were trying out a new type of homemade grenade and boom, boom, boom! Tita and Ruth went running out again. Why don't they listen?

I finished my drawing. It's a great success. Even I must admit that it's quite good. Chevo is crazy about it and wants to take it to show Susana. I think I'll keep it with me. Anybody wants to see it they'll have to come here. It was something to concentrate on for a couple of days.

War story: A combatant hadn't seen himself in a mirror for over a year. One day he walked into someone's house and saw a uniformed *compa* standing by the wall. He immediately saluted and said 'Buenos días compa.' He felt like a complete fool when he realized he had saluted his image in the mirror.

Tita is back and the haircutting business is going full force. You see, our hotel even offers a beauty salon. She is very good and cuts each person's hair differently. People come from all around, even Douglas dropped by for a haircut.

After the haircut they ask to see the drawing – beauty salon and art gallery here.

Chevo brought Susana over just to look at the drawing. She liked it and then asked what was happening with my exit. I told her what I knew: that when Esteban left someone else would. . . that he had not. . . no one had. . . and I felt it was very disrespectful on their part. She said that she would be seeing Esteban – he's back – tonight and I would hear from him tomorrow.

Crazy Toño and calm Sergio came by with a letter from Elias, head of the radio, asking me to give them all the unexposed film I had. Not even a hello, thanks or anything. I gave them 18 rolls, just about all that I have and wrote that that was it as I had already given over 20 rolls these last four months to Julio and Toño.

Esteban came by this afternoon. Great to see him. First thing he asked was to see 'the famous drawing'. He liked it a lot. Then he said that they hadn't decided yet what would be the best way to get me out. He said not to worry, something would be arranged, but he had the feeling that I would have to wait another month. He asked me what would interest me, what I would like to learn more about, since I might as well do something during this month. I agreed completely, but I was not prepared for this, so I told him I would have to think about it.

A *compa* dropped off some of his poems for me to read. I've done a little editing on the three I like best. His name is Alberto and they were written in 1983:

Our guerrilla life
is a love poem
a love poem written in blood

from battles, from anonymous mutilated corpses
appearing at dawn by the side of the road
our guerrilla life
is a love poem
of pure love.

That's it, that's it
shoot
the smell of gunpowder
will be our perfume
shoot
shoot
let us shout to the world
that this is the moment
when the guerrilla
loves with the most intensity
shoot *compa*!

I have not died
there I am
there is my body
growing in the weeds
in the trees
there I am
there is my body
in each atom
of the minerals of the earth
there I am
there is my blood
in the nectar of the flowers
that the wild birds drink
there I am
there is my love
in the sweetness
of the children's laughter
there I am
there are my hopes
in the hands of the workers
there I am
there is my conviction
in the flag
blowing free
there I am

there is my history
in every trench
there I am
there in the heart of my people.

It is 28 June and at 02:00 hrs the FMLN attacked the Cerrón Grande Dam, the largest hydroelectric dam in Central America. It is now 07:00 hrs and the dam is completely under FMLN control.

This military operation has been called *'Viva las heróicas luchas de los trabajadores– derrotemos el intreguismo de Duarte'* ('Hurrah for the workers' heroic fights/let us defeat Duarte's sellout). The workers they refer to are the ones who have been on strike throughout the country. The strikers are testing Duarte's electoral promises. By giving the operation this title, the FMLN is showing its support for the workers and their demands.

It is now noon and the *compas* have deserted the dam.

I am extremely pissed off that I wasn't there. Sometimes I think I'm here for the mountain air. I'm so pissed off that I sent a note to Esteban saying: the enemy didn't allow the foreign press near the dam, how come the FMLN did the same? All that film I gave – that's what it was for. And do they invite me? Hell!

The dam was built in 1972. During its construction a lot of data was printed as to its design, height of mountains surrounding it, distances, etc., which, I assume, the *compas* got copies of. They built 33 guardhouses around it, a barracks and a little town for the workers. The FMLN strategy was to hit everything at once (except the town) and move in.

Several hours before the attack the FMLN Special Forces penetrated the zone and set up artillery aimed at the guardhouses and the barracks. All artillery had to be aimed with precision as there were going to be *compas* inside the line of fire.

Julio walked with the first troops who were going to storm the dam. Hundreds of *compas* walked during the evening and converged near the dam. Throughout their quiet walk reconnaissance planes flew all around (I don't understand how these planes can't detect a massive movement of troops). At the same time, all roads leading to the dam were taken. The storming troops moved up the hill and silently passed the 33 guardhouses surrounding the periphery of the dam.

Julio, who was to photograph the initial operation, said they penetrated the circle of guardhouses and waited. At exactly 02:00 hrs the Special Forces started off the artillery and left. For eight minutes the place was popping with mortars. Thirty-two of the 33 guardhouses and the barracks blew up simultaneously. Julio said it was an incredible sight. He was sitting high up. First there were all the lights from the mortars going off and then hundreds of M-16s, on automatic, moving into the center towards the barracks. 'Like a luminous flower closing up', he said. In 15 minutes they had control of the dam and hundreds of government soldiers were lying dead everywhere.

Sergio recorded the sound of the whole battle and of all radio communication between the government forces and between the *compas* (something the FMLN does whenever possible) while he sat in the command post. He said that the confusion and chaos within the dam was so extreme that it was the other dam, the Fifth of November Dam, that radioed the command headquarters in San Salvador, saying they heard commotion and firing at the Cerrón Grande. It took time to get a plane, as the honchos in San Salvador were not at all concerned. When the plane finally arrived at 04:00 hrs and circled over the dam, the pilot radioed in 'looks perfectly quiet and normal here but I'll send out a flare just to make sure.' When the flare went out the pilot yelled, 'Good God! The place is blown to bits!'

At 05:00 hrs the Salvadoran military was sending all the forces they could to the dam but the roads were blocked by the FMLN and they couldn't get through. Headquarters called in troops stationed in the town of Chalatenango to come over the mountains but the area was mined and the troops refused to advance. An officer killed a soldier for refusing but the troops still refused and returned to their barracks.

Toño, who was to film the next stage, arrived with the troops that took over once the place was secure. There was little he could film except bodies. He was very upset. 'I've never seen so many dead. The *compas* really killed a lot of people there.' (Total casualties were 500 – mostly dead.)

By 10:00 hrs the *compas* had left the dam – it was completely empty. By noon the government forces had regained the dam. One of the first soldiers to enter the dam radioed to the high command: 'There are a hell of a lot of dead here. What are we going to do? And they're all naked!' While the government forces were trying to recapture an empty dam the *compas* were bathing, eating and resting. Pretty incredible. No?

The taking of the Cerrón Grande Dam was, according to the FMLN, a victory on several levels. Obviously, a military victory, and one in which four of the five groups that make up the FMLN participated (first time during a major operation). Politically it was also a victory in that it showed the masses that the FMLN was with them in their demands, not only in spirit but in might as well. They took the most guarded government place just to make a statement to the Salvadorans and to Duarte: 'We are a major force that you will have to contend with and if you are talking about negotiations it is with us, armed, that you will talk.'

It will go down as one of the historic battles in the history of this war and I wish I had been there. Not counting the killing, it was a spectacular operation.

It was even more spectacular than the taking of the Paraíso garrison – north of the town of Chalatenango, designed and built by the US military, surrounded by open, dry fields providing no cover in its approach. I am told that the US military would fly in by helicopter, once a month, to show off their untakeable garrison. On 30 December, 1983, it was taken by the FMLN.

In a matter of minutes they had the place surrounded and under their control. They had trucks outside waiting to be filled up with weapons, clothing and ammunition. When they finally had to leave they had not taken a fifth of what was stored there. Francisco, the doctor, said that there were layers and layers of storage underground and when they left they decided to blow up what they couldn't take. He said they almost blew themselves up because they didn't realize the quantity of ammo still there.

I think the *compas* are extraordinary combatants.

July

It's a beautiful evening and I'm feeling homesick. Not for a place but for friends, family, the world out there. I feel very cut off here. I'm tired of relating to a notebook and to a few people during rare moments. I want to feel that I'm a human being too, with needs, desires and dreams. Now it's getting dark, I have no candle and I'm all alone in this house. Twelve hours of darkness to live through, sleep through, wait through.

I went for a stroll in the mountains this morning and thought about peasants again, about the difference in worlds, in sensitivity.

For example, I always get pissed off that people stare at me when I write. They make a point of sitting next to me so that they can watch. It irritates me because it breaks my concentration and invades my privacy. But they are totally unaware of my irritation and the reasons for it. How could they be aware? People who are left-handed (which I am) are rare. People who can write are rarer. People who are left-handed and write for long periods of time, off the top of their heads, are weird. What does this weird left-handed woman write about? Blank. To imagine what I am writing is not imaginable. But it's worth watching this person doing it.

People who want to be left alone to do such things are also incomprehensible. Privacy is a luxury peasants can't afford. Privacy and writing belong to another class from theirs, it is not part of their world.

Second example. When I first arrived here and was taken to what would be my base for several months I thought it very inconsiderate that no one sort of welcomed me, told me about the layout of the land, about the store, and especially, about the outhouse. Why didn't they? Not because they were being thoughtless, but because to do so would reflect a middle-class upbringing. No? Especially the hole in the ground. As I soon discovered, a number of people in *Propa* didn't even use it. They shat wherever the beans moved them.

Actually, it's the only one I've encountered these four months. So what I took as unfriendly was/is cultural, class difference. Nobody 'showed me the bathroom' because most of them don't know or care what a bathroom is.

Third example. My inability to understand how these people can sit around doing nothing for such long periods of time. My irritation watching the children who have nothing to stimulate their minds and the adults seemingly not much concerned with them or their own minds. The exasperation I feel when I have nothing to do and no stimulation. Again, I am a product of another class, another world. I have had the luxury of being brought up extremely well nourished and in a dynamic and stimulating environment. Peasants have not. There is nothing dynamic or stimulating about poverty.

To expect them to come home after working like a beast in the fields all day, bursting with energy and ideas, sit under the light of a candle and invent an intricate machine that will eat fleas is to be totally insensitive and ignorant.

In this tiny country I have met people who have never left the area they were born in. I have met people who have never seen the ocean. I have met people who if they think about it, would say, have said, 'I guess the world is flat.'

What I have, a peasant can't imagine. What I take for granted he/she cannot understand. Can Americans understand the depths of their poverty?

So much for my stroll in the mountains.

Eva's *compa* died in the taking of the dam. Poor Eva. This is her second *compa* to die in the war.

Manuel also died. I'm very sad. He was a lovely person, gentle and kind. He used to be with the Atlacatl (the elite government battalion) then joined the guerrillas and was a commando in the FES.

They are having a big party in Ojos de Agua to celebrate the success of the Cerrón Grande operation. I would like to go but I am told that there are too many 'ears' there if I am leaving soon. I shall sit here calmly and watch the clouds go by.

When the organization was young and puritanical, you couldn't drink (drinking is still not allowed in the zones), couldn't smoke (unless you were hooked like Douglas), couldn't be an active Christian, couldn't think about abortions (seemingly contradictory, no?). When they first started having dances for the troops some of the old-timers thought it was wrong – this was a war, not a party. Anyway, those were in the pure days when revolution was all theory. Now with practise it has become more human and tolerant.

The more I listen to the Farabundo radio the more I don't like it. When it deals with battles, it is very good, especially the big ones. But I think it would be of interest if after these battles they discussed them in terms of their importance, their implications, on a peasant/worker level. But they only focus on the battle itself.

Compas listen to the radio because they want to know what is happening militarily and also because it's *their* radio. But once that particular information is over it becomes background noise. Guillermo has a strong professional voice but the tone is always the same – it's too professional – it goes on and on and eventually you stop paying attention. The songs they play are also repetitive. They should have new songs and songs that peasants can understand.

Rosario was telling me that a year ago when she started working with peasants, they didn't understand her when she spoke. Sure they understood her Spanish – she's Salvadoran – but they didn't understand what she meant, she was not connecting with them. I feel the radio is the same: it does not connect with these people. And I don't think it connects with the combatants. When I was with the X-21 most of the kids tuned into a rock and roll station. If news came on they changed stations or turned it off. Plus the kids who have radios only have AM, they don't have shortwave. So who is the radio reaching?

Esteban should go back to making speeches. I am told that he is famous throughout the country and a fantastic speaker. His real name is Facundo Guardado. How about a little passion on the radio, once in a while, Esteban?

I guess I'll go to Zapotal and get more batteries for my tape recorder. Chevo was kind enough to give me a funky old typewriter and I'm transcribing my interviews. Something to do. Off I go.

In Zapotal I met one of Susana's bodyguards. He waited while I bought my things. I said he didn't have to but he did anyway. When we got to the section of the mountain which separates from the road, he left me. A few hours later, while I was transcribing, I received a note from the *Comité Zonal* telling me that I was not to go to town by myself because it was not safe. Either I send someone to get what I need or I go with an armed *compa*. Yes, ma'am.

It's a beautiful day, full of sunshine. It's the fifteenth and I'm told that it won't rain for two weeks. This is the period when they will harvest the corn and beans. I have four rolls of film left so I should shoot the harvest one of these days.

Chevo brought Meme and David over from the X-21 to see the drawing. Meme, the political head of the X-21, sang the chant 'Yankee aggressor, out of El Salvador' and added 'but Taina can stay.' Thank you, but I think I'd like to go.

Met Roberto, a South American, also waiting to get out. He's been here three years studying the military aspect of the war. He said he had learned a lot. Then he started laughing and said that in the camp he is staying in there is a new Swiss internationalist. It seems that the Swiss is very upset because the *compas* throw their dead batteries in the bushes. He is trying to explain to everyone that batteries are bad for the plants! In Switzerland you put them in a bag and take them somewhere special. Ah, yes, the meeting of two worlds.

I've decided that I want to go back to the Felipe front. I want to understand how a war is fought in such a tiny country with the enemy close by – how battles are designed and won. Meme is going with a group in that direction day after tomorrow so I've written to Esteban asking if I can go along.

The hotel is full of friends and others. The number of people who come and go through this place and all the others I've seen throughout my stay here, all doing a variety of jobs, makes me understand that the 'guerrilla', the combatant him/herself, is just one part of the FMLN.

Esteban came by to tell me that I cannot go to Felipe; that a decision will be made soon and Felipe is too far and too dangerous at the moment. OK, I understand what it means to be 'awaiting', it means just that. Hell.

He then apologized for my not having gone to the taking of the dam. He forgot about me because he was so busy. 'I simply forgot and I'm sorry.' I told him that he owed me a big one. He smiled, 'OK, I owe you one.' In exchange for not being able to go to Felipe he offered the K-23 battalion stationed in the north of Chalate. They will be going on a special assignment and I could accompany them. I don't know. North of Chalate means a hell of a mountainous walk and I don't know that I'm up for staying with a new group, where I don't know anybody again.

Well, here I am with the K-23. Arrived yesterday. It wasn't as bad as I thought. We got a ride in a jeep and ended up walking only four hours. The ups were not bad, and now I'm sitting on a mountain covered with pine trees and looking out to new mountains. It's very pretty and quite cool at night. Unlike the X-21, this battalion is more stationary. They go off on some operations but mostly their function is (I think) to deal with government forces should they enter the zone.

This area is still part of the controlled zone but further north and called La Dos (The Two). Where I have been based is called La Una (The One). La Dos has a number of larger towns where the government forces send troops to spend the night or stay a couple of days and then leave. So it is a mixed zone with some towns quietly pro-FMLN, others openly pro, and other large towns are considered areas of expansion with the work done semi-clandestinely.

I'm with the military command of La Dos and I'm sitting in a tent-like construction. It's raining and the drops plop on the canvas and it's gloomy, cold and dismal. There is absolutely nothing to do but sit here in the gloomy plopping tent. Those who have more 'educated' minds are in other areas, with *compas* somewhat like them or moving around doing this or that. Me, I sit here doing nothing. The others, the majority, have nowhere to go, nothing else to do and they are in no hurry. If they were not with the FMLN, what would they be doing?

In a country torn by war and violence there are not too many options for the poor teenagers of El Salvador. Unemployment in the cities and countryside is very high. If you have no schooling or just a couple of years, there is no future for you other than toiling in the fields (if work is available) for a barely livable wage. If you make it to highschool or through it there aren't many jobs on the market. You can leave the country and go hang around in a refugee camp, but there is no future there. If you hang around inside the country inevitably you will get picked up by the government forces and be forced to fight for them. Life itself offers little promise, so you join the guerrillas as a way out, because you can fight back, because you are part of something, of a group, and they are your generation.

This tent is packed with people, one half giggling and the other half sleeping. Time passes, another night, another day, another month will come. The year 1985 is on its way and the war will continue until it's won and that's that. It's in motion, it has its own rhythm, it will not be stopped. The slow dance of revolution.

I discovered that Eva is down the mountain working with the *Comité* of this zone. I went to visit her and see how she's doing after her *compa* died. She still has her wonderful laugh and said, 'I'm glad he died fighting rather than die miserably and defeated like so many before the war.'

I've decided to get out of here. I've had enough. Neto, military head of this zone, told me that they are going on a 'job' in three days.

'How long a walk?'

'Half a day and all night.'

'What kind of battle?'

'We're going to ambush some troops.'

'Is it going to be in the mountains, jumping in and out of foliage?'

'Yes.'

Then it's unphotographable. Walking in the dark is the worst thing for my feet and, anyway, I've lost the spirit. I'm not going to walk three days to shoot nothing.

There is a train of mules – moving supplies – leaving at 10:00 hrs tomorrow and connecting with a jeep at 14:00 hrs. I'm going with them instead.

The train left on time and it was quite a walk. Beautiful because we were so high and the view was great. The mountains are a bitch but beautiful. There we were walking through the mountains with ten mules laden with bullets, four armed *compas* and myself in broad daylight. The bullets were in produce bags, their points sticking out all over so if anybody wanted to know what they were carrying it was quite obvious. We walked through little towns, the sun was shining and all was peaceful. A walk with the mules in the countryside, except that there is a war and the mules are carrying pounds of bullets.

It was strange walking by the little farms and towns, the people looking at us and not saying anything. I had the feeling of what I believe exists in many places in this country: that quiet support for the FMLN without which they couldn't have gotten as far as they have. The country is just too small to walk around with mules and bullets and armed *compas* and buy the quantities they do, if they don't have a network and the support of part of the population.

We finally arrived at the outskirts of a town where the jeep was waiting for us. We drove to La Laguna and parked on a little street to wait until dark. The driver told me that we had to wait because they had bought 150 pairs of boots and the store owner didn't want any 'ears' seeing that many boots leaving his store. At 20:00 hrs we left with the jeep stuffed with boots and cartridges.

I have arranged to shoot the harvest on Wednesday. Hope my feet make it. I'll go half way to Tamarindo tomorrow, visit Tita and spend the night. I definitely have the feeling that I will be leaving end of the month. Carlos thinks so too. So I'm finishing things up and saying good-bye to the *compas*.

I went to Soila's, the woman with the little store, and saw a filthy little girl sitting in the mud, her hands and face covered with the mud. Soila handed out candy to all of us and her mother watched as the kid ate it, licking her hands and sucking her fingers. She didn't bat an eye. In contrast, there is a woman working with AMES, staying at my hotel, and her little girl is very clean. If she is left alone she is penned in, sitting on a clean cloth on the ground so she can't come into contact with the dirt floor. There is so much work to do here. As Tilo (the priest) said, 'It is harder to educate one generation than to fight a war of liberation.'

A musical group from the FAL, called Tepehuani – five Salvadoran men – has entered the country recently (they live in Europe) and is travelling around the different fronts. They gave a concert at Sonia's, who takes care of the military dispensary just down the mountain. They have come to learn about the war so as to improve their revolutionary sense and therefore songs.

Their last song had a fast beat and they began to dance, asking for women to join them. Salvadorans, being typically shy, refused, so they came to me and I accepted. Everyone got very excited and started clapping and yelling. Me, a *gringa*, having to represent the Salvadoran women.

There is another invasion in Felipe and another massacre of civilians by the Atlacatl. The only rationalization I can make about why the most elite battalion of the Salvadoran army kills civilians is frustration. They are the best trained troops, trained in the art of killing (rather like a lesser developed version of the Marines) and the people they are supposed to kill – the guerrillas – they rarely see. So, I guess, they take their anger and frustration out on the civilian population.

Sergio came by on his way to somewhere. He told me that one of the areas he is working in is Salvadoran culture: what is it, how does it manifest itself, how can it be developed? He is taking an inventory so that they will have something to work on after the war. Interesting. 'Even the way you eat is cultural,' he said.

'I think the way you fight a war is also cultural', I said.

Well, it's definitely a beautiful day for bombing. Visibility is excellent. Everything is green, clean and shiny. An A-37 came by and threw out some bombs, then another plane came by and threw out propaganda. This time it was printed *colon* bills, made to look like Salvadoran money, offering 3,000 *colones* for a 120mm cannon. On the other side was a drawing of the cannon in case you don't know what it looks like or can't read. It's not the kind of thing one would throw over one's shoulder and saunter off to a garrison to exchange for money, now, is it folks?

Felix from, what I call, the political/ideological *mara*, dropped by for a visit. He said that, except for the Vietnamese, no other guerrilla war has used political, military and economic strategy the way the FMLN does. I'm not exactly sure what he means by this, but I think he is saying that the FMLN is far more involved, on many levels throughout the country, in both rural and urban areas, than people may think or wish. I think it would be impossible to take a poll here in this country, as Americans do about everything in their society, in order to find out how many are on which side. After the extreme repression and violence of the 1970s I doubt anyone is going to say what they really believe.

Actually, my sense of the Salvadoran people is that they do not freely speak their minds to just anybody. I think that peasants, especially, are the last to tell you what they think. I find Salvadoran peasants to be a stubborn breed. A stubbornness that comes from the hardness of the land they work on, the hardness of their lives. Misery has bred stubbornness, and because of this they are not easily influenced by others. They do not trust others on principle, and so to reach them, to get them involved, is not done overnight, neither is it done from the outside. I think peasants listen very sharply, keep their mouths shut, and go off and think about what they have heard. If and when they decide on something, it will be done with the same stubbornness as everything else in their lives. This tenacity, once they become fighters – in the large sense of the word – makes them a formidable and, perhaps, incomprehensible enemy. The school of life molds the guerrilla, and if they are peasants, beware, O middle class, because theirs is a strength that bombs and bullets cannot destroy.

How wide and how deep is the infrastructure of this revolution? From what I understand so far there are the silent pro, the sympathizers, the collaborators, the openly pro, the FMLN itself with all its various people. But how many is that? Just to clothe and feed, organize and maneuver a whole brigade only 25 to 30 kilometers from the capital, which is the headquarters of the Salvadoran military with its US advisors, its A-37s, its Hughes UH-1 helicopters, and now its AC-47 gunships. How does the FMLN do it?

Felix asked me if I understood something about this war, because he said that sometimes he doesn't. When you consider all the years of poverty, the years spent organizing, demonstrating, striking, and the constant repression, and now creating an army, which means that on top of the daily struggle to survive, they have to live with bombing and mortar attacks, battles and invasions. 'How do these people have the energy to go on and on?' Felix asked.

I said I thought that, to a certain extent, their lifestyle now, although a continuation of the poverty and suffering of the past, holds the promise of a new life. Perhaps war could represent the possible escape from poverty, and anyway, what have they to lose? No? He said yes.

The Farabundo has confirmed that 62 civilians were killed on the 19th and 22nd by the Atlacatl during the invasion in Felipe. Mostly young kids and old people. Doesn't it bother them that all they can kill are children and old people?

The *compas* ambushed three companies in San Vicente – more guns, more prisoners. The exact figures are not known yet. The FMLN has informed the government and the cotton growers that cotton does not fill the belly; since the government is importing basic grain they will sabotage all attempts to continue with the cotton cultivation.

A little town near Tamarindo was hit with eight bombs yesterday. The four I saw were actually five but the fifth did not explode. When this happens, which seems to be quite frequently, the *compas* send their explosives experts who de-activate the bomb, take it apart and use the explosives to make grenades and mines.

I photographed the harvest. I think I got some good shots although my film is oozing with humidity and probably covered with fungus. I am oozing with sweat and many people here have fungus growing on their feet. It has to do with wearing polyester socks, if they wear socks, and wet boots. I've seen feet without toenails because of the fungus and they tell me that it itches like hell. I still have my wool socks and my great boots, so my feet are fine except when I walk, which is a whole other matter.

I'm glad that I've never had to stay too long near the Sumpul River. It's unbearably hot and the air is thick with moisture and mosquitoes. I met the head of production and went with ten peasants to the corn fields. The corn is now full grown and beginning to dry. They bend the stalks so that the tips of the ears are pointing downwards allowing the water to roll off and they will leave it there to dry for another month. They are hard-working men and proud of what they have planted. They planted 22 *manzanas* (around twelve acres) for the *compas* and three for themselves. They expect to harvest 220 pounds of beans for the *compas* and 60 for themselves. The fish cooperative on a good day catches 50–70 fish. Most of it goes to the hospital for the sick and wounded.

I left for Tamarindo at 15:30 hrs. Pure pain in the feet. I definitely want to exchange them for a new pair – these aren't any good at all. On the way, Jorge, the nurse, came up behind me. I've not seen him since our confrontation in the hospital. He asked me if I had made it to Felipe, and then said that he has never been to any of the areas where the major battles have been fought, has never worked with an active battalion, always been with the rearguard and worked with the civilian population. He likes it here. 'In the vanguard they are taking power, in the rearguard they are making the revolution,' he said.

He's been here a year and a half and seems to have a great deal of respect for the peasants. He's tall and thin – but then every foreigner here loses their fat, if they have any, in a few months – with blond, blond hair and green eyes. He told me that a few months after arriving in Chalate he went off, on his own, to a little hamlet to check out the people's health problems. Since he was still very new, most people didn't know him, so when this tall, white, blond appeared walking down the side of the mountain the people in the hamlet yelled out, 'The *gringos* are coming!' Everybody grabbed sticks, stones, machetes, whatever they could find, and went to meet the *gringo* invasion. They surrounded him, and sent a messenger to find out who he was. What touches me about this story is that the whole little town with their sticks and stones were willing to confront the *gringos*, not knowing if this meant one man or 20, armed or unarmed.

I'm back in Cordoncillo. Last night in Tamarindo Betio and Francisco made me a real dinner: rice with vegetables, fried fish, cucumbers, coffee and bread. At midnight I woke up with a horrible stomach ache. My body can't take real food. This morning I had diarrhea but I will survive. It took me four hours to get from there to here. God, I cannot walk.

Tilo came by in the evening for a visit. He's a good man. Forever walking all over this country, meeting people, helping people, giving mass, organizing this and that. The roving priest with his black hat, his sweat-filled beard and his twinkling eyes. He said that running a revolutionary war was like running a government: the variety of jobs and people needed to do the jobs, the economics involved, the social, political and educational work, the coordination and keeping track of it all while fighting.

He spoke of the FPL and how in the beginning, when you join, your first job is a test to find out who you are, what you think, how much you're willing to give. You have to give all and be open, and talk about everything that goes through your mind, because this is your new family; and you have to be clear, and you have to be sure, and you have to be trustworthy. Without all these three the organization can't afford you, not now that the battle for power is well on its way. After the triumph there will be many degrees of relationships that can and will develop, but not now.

And, continued Tilo, the revolutions that succeed are the simple ones. Should a science fiction writer come here to write a novel, he/she would write about a simple primitive folk defeating an advanced technological folk.

I think there are many truths being lived and fought for here. And they are simple truths. I don't think that truth is a fixed or rigid concept. I think it has its own history, its own time, its own people. What is 'their' truth may not be 'our' truth. But that doesn't make it less true, does it?

August

Tita is here for a couple of days. She just finished giving a week's course to the Popular Power Presidents. It ranged from geography and math to how to organize themselves and their localities. Tita is a born teacher and has worked with the Mexican poor and peasants for many years. At the end of the course she asked them to write what they thought of it, make a drawing that showed how they used to feel and how they feel now, and write a short paragraph on what has been the most important event in their lives.

She showed me her favorite drawing: the paper was divided into two, on the left was a drawing of a tree that was also a man, all dried up, hunched over, standing on barren land. On the right was the same tree/man erect, with leaves and bearing fruit. By the side was a house and people and a big sun shining. The man who drew it said that the dried up tree was the way he felt in the past but now that he is organized and working in the revolution he feels like a tall, leafy, fruit-bearing tree.

I then read what had been the most important event in their lives. These are men who have just learned to read and write or have had one year of schooling as children. Here are excerpts of two that I liked:

> The biggest impressions has been the first time that I road in buses – because I didn't know them and today grown-up to know the ignorance in which I found myself and the good thing is when you keep on finding out.

> For me the most impressive is to know that they cheated us because of our ignorance feeling that we were nothing next to the powerful but now it impresses me more to know that we have the opportunity to learn.

Tita said it was an incredible experience to spend a week with them. They were so open about their ignorance and they wanted so much to learn. She said it was 'Why, why, and why' all the time. I know what she is talking about. I've experienced this in Nicaragua, in Brazil and during the sub-regional elections here in April. To see people changing as their minds become alive, the excitement that comes from learning and from having a certain power over their own lives and participating in a community effort. That's when the word 'revolution' makes my heart go thump, thump.

The gifts of knowledge and participation. What greater gifts can one give a people? Not to hand it on a platter, which is impossible, but to help and encourage the development of a society where people can proceed in their own way. Not my way, not your way, in their way.

At the end of the course Tita talked about the universe, that the planet was round, that there was more than one sun and many other worlds. They were absolutely fascinated. Several came up to her later and said that the most impressive thing in their lives to date was knowing that there was more than one sun.

It's a beautiful day. The green is getting thicker and taller, Roberto Carlos sings love songs and a *compa* or two slip by in the mud, or one stops, bathed in sweat, for a drink of water or a bath. And me? What to do with all I feel, all I've learned? How to give it – how to create the bridge? There is more than one sun, the earth is round and this is their revolution.

In El Salvador, between the mass organizations and the picking up of guns, there was a bridge, and that bridge, I think, was the deathsquads and repression mixed with their history. The bridge in Nicaragua? Somoza himself. In Guatemala? The bridges of history, you blow them up, you build them, you separate, you unite.

I went to a remembrance party down at Sonia's. Sonia runs the military supply store for the battalion of logistics and supplies. The occasion was to remember the death of a *compa* from that battalion killed last year during a government invasion. Juan, one of the heads of the battalion, gave a short speech about Luis, the man who had died.

He talked about the man himself and then about death. How death is not something strange or new to the Salvadoran people. That they are accustomed to death, to children dying of hunger and disease, parents dying of old age at 35 or 40, people dying simply because they're poor, because they ask for a ten-cent increase for their labor. But who remembered those deaths? Their mothers, brothers, husbands, but always an individual remembrance. 'But now', Juan said, 'death has a meaning and belongs to all of us who struggle. Luis's death and the others who have fallen since the war began have made dying meaningful, an act of hope. In that sense they never die, they become part of our life in our struggle to create a new one.'

The Tepehuani began to play, they passed out Kool-aid and bread, and people danced.

'They don't drink coffee where you come from, do they?'
'Oh yes, coffee yes. Just about everybody drinks coffee.'
'Really? They drink coffee there too?'
'Yes, but we don't eat tortillas.'
'You don't eat tortillas?'
'No, we eat bread.'
'No! No tortillas? My God!'
'Tortillas are only eaten in Central America and Mexico.'

What does Central America or Mexico mean to her? She has never seen the ocean, never been to the capital, never talked on a phone. What does Central America mean? A word used to describe something that she hears a lot of these days, these years of listening to the Farabundo. What does El Salvador mean to her? Her house, garden, family, her deaths, this war. This is what she knows, this she understands. Even Nicaragua – another word she has heard during the war – but what does it mean? What image comes to mind? None of it fits within her experience of life lived in these rugged mountains. And she is a *compa*, she has the Popular Store down the mountain.

'And chickens, do you eat chickens over there?'

'Yes.'

'Your mother must have many of them in her yard. No?'

'Well, actually, where I live the chickens we eat we buy in a store, all cut up and wrapped in plastic.'

Frown.

I don't tell her that many people over there have never seen live chickens even though they eat them.

'And your boots? They're not from here. They're from where you live?'

'No, they're from Italy.'

Another word that means nothing to her. Italy? Her hazel eyes open wide as she looks at me. Whatever I'm talking about it is not Salvadoran. It is out there, another strange word that this foreigner uses among so many others. It passes quickly, this lack of meaning. Gone in a flash, if it flashed at all. And she rolls the stone grinding the *maizillo* to make tortillas. Tortillas, yes, that is hers, that is her world and totally comprehensible.

Just as her mind draws a blank upon my world so does my world draw a blank upon the intensity of their poverty. Two worlds that have never met. The bridge, where is the goddamn bridge?

My world in the evening goes like this: I brush my teeth in the bushes and then take my cover out of my knapsack and walk over to my hammock. I place the cover in the hammock and, standing, I step out of my boots, one at a time to take off my jeans, careful to put my foot back into my boot as the dirt floor is covered with fleas. I shake my jeans, turn them inside out and shake them some more to get rid of any fleas. Quickly I put them back on trying not to let them touch the ground, and jump into the hammock. Then I take my socks off and with the flashlight cradled in my neck I check each one very carefully, inside and out for fleas. I usually find some and squish them, others jump off during the search. I put them back on, turn out the flashlight and put it into my boot directly below me. I take my cover and begin the slow awkward dance of tucking myself in. I start with my feet, tucking tightly, up, up, as the hammock sways, until I get to my head and shoulders. Then I bend my arms inside and stretch the rest of the cover over my head and around my shoulders. I have just enough stretch to push my arms down to my sides. I am tucked in. The bats begin to stretch and flap their wings preparing for their night outings.

I turn from a fetal position on my left – or as close as I can get into one in a hammock – to one on my right which means readjusting my tucked-in cover.

Then I go from right to straight, also readjusting the cover and the thin ropes holding my thin hammock twang with each movement.

I cannot sleep. I pull out a cigarette and matches from my shirt pocket, uncover my head with bent arms and shove my arms up and out, emerging from my cocoon, and light the thing. The match falls to the ground and for a couple of seconds there is a faint light. The fleas become the focus. Each tiny movement of their tiny legs I can feel and – zap – I go for it. Squeezing the hell out of a small area of my bluejeans. The force and concentration I use just to kill a flea. I inhale on my cigarette again, waiting to see if I got it or not. Half the time there isn't any more tickling across my skin and the other half it waits a little and then on it moves to another juicy area. The dance and contradance of the fleas on my body. When I turn in one direction they creep over, ever so delicately, to the other side. I finish my cigarette, shove my arms back inside, cover my head and move into the next position.

This is how I spend my nights. A dance of positions, fleas, cigarettes, all in darkness, and my mind jumping like the fleas over the body of my past, present and future. And how many more of these nights must I dance through? This lonely dance in the darkness of the warring mountains of El Salvador?

This place has ceased being a hotel. Now it's a drop-off point for people going and coming. This afternoon a guy appeared who joined the FMLN last month and just got out of the *escuelita*.

'Why did you join now at 26 years of age and not before?'

'Well, where we lived it was very controlled, very repressive. Then we went to the capital. I have a sister in Los Angeles who sends us money for food.'

'What were you doing in the capital?'

'Oh, nothing. Then I was helping to make deliveries in a truck around here and talked to some *compas* and they brought me here. I know there is injustice in my country and so I've come to fight.'

'But there's been injustice here for years. Why now and not before?'

He does not answer. He has nothing, not even a knapsack, just the clothes on his body. There must be a reason for joining, but what is it?

'I have two cousins that are fighting here. I don't know if they are alive or where they are.'

'And does your family know you are here?'

'Oh, no.'

'You just left?'

'Yes.'

'What must they think?'

'Oh, probably that I'm dead.'

'So, what do you think of all this?'

'Oh, I think it's lovely.'

Lovely?

'But why now and not before?'

'*Pues sí*, we were sleeping, we didn't have any awareness.'

'Yes, but I'm talking about you not we.'

'Yes, me, my family. I'm not educated, we're very poor, we work the land but there is no land.'

'So, what – you just decided to join?'

'Yes, I just decided.'

He just decided. Why should it be more complicated? What else is there to do? Thousands of young people in this country without anything to do, without job opportunities, and, so, like they said in Felipe, either you're picked up by the army or you go with the *compas*.

The *compas* come and go, up and down, carrying or not, knapsacks or none, always on the move, getting something, going somewhere. Others sitting doing nothing, others counting cartridges or sheets of paper. Inventory, always inventory. Sonia spent the night counting 21,000 bullets. Must count, must divide, must distribute and must always go searching for more. It is never enough. The mouths to feed, the bodies to clothe, the feet to boot, the arms to arm, so much and so much more that I am not aware of. The day to day of operating, living and fighting a war.

I came here to experience a war with all that the imagination creates with that word and what I have experienced is a people, a people at war. And it has its bang-bangs, its bombs and death, but it has so much more that, without this so much more, this war would not be possible. And I have not been able to capture even half of it on film, but I know it, I have learned it.

Luis, the Spaniard, came by and said, 'So, you're still around here, eh? I thought you were supposed to be out of here by now!'

Who, me? I'm the photographer/writer-in-residence of the front.

Just watched two A-37s drop ten bombs on the other side of the mountain, near the river. They really upset me. The day the FMLN can shoot those planes down will be a fine day indeed.

They say, 'Ah, but the guerrillas come from the people.' Of course they come from the people. Where do the government soldiers come from, machines? Does that mean that one has the right to bomb any town in the US because the war advisors come from the US? Of course not. You can't bomb the civilian population.

A *compa* called Andrés came by from La Tres. La Tres is further north from La Dos and is a zone of expansion. He's been working in expansion for five months. Before that he was with the X-21, from the taking of Cinquera to the taking of Paraíso. He developed very bad ulcers and was moved into expansion.

I asked him to tell me about the people in La Tres. We had been talking about food, about tortillas of *maizillo*. He said they are surprised when you tell them that here in the controlled zone people farm collectively and they don't understand why people eat *maizillo* here – only animals do. They see the *compas* buying in large quantities and it seems a contradiction – why eat animal food?

He told me that before the *compas* started coming around the people thought the guerrillas were big, tall, black, bearded Cubans with big feet. When the *compas* began appearing they would hide in their houses. Now they are very friendly, invite you to eat, sleep, etc. A *compa* might come into town and start talking to a couple of people on the street and soon there is a large group surrounding the *compa* wanting to hear what he/she is saying. As their presence increases the people see how well mannered they are and begin to make comparisons between the *compas'* behavior and that of the soldiers when they come to town. The soldiers, according to them, are arrogant, machista, vulgar and intimidating.

Even though the people see that the *compas* are just like them they are in awe of them. They don't understand that the *compas* didn't start uniformed and well-armed.

'We don't like to use the word guerrilla, sounds bad.'

'Well, guerrilla signifies a military way of fighting.'

'Yes, but it sounds bad, we'll call you *muchachos*.'

Often when talking to Andrés they say, 'Well, after the triumph which garrison are you going to live in?' They don't understand that most of the *compas* are fighting because it is necessary and that after the triumph they will do very different things.

Andrés thinks of the guerrilla as being similar to a doctor – like a vocation that is part of an historical/social process that one does for the people, for the future and then, after one wins, one moves into the next stage of social responsibility.

Then he told me that during the April elections, the only party up there seeking votes was the PDC (Duarte's party). They would hand out propaganda and run around in cars with loudspeakers at the same time that the *compas* were in town. The PDC would use certain FMLN terms and the people confused Duarte with the FMLN. One of them, after the elections, said to Andrés, 'Well, now things should get better for you because your man won.'

In terms of recruitment, Andrés believes that the *compas* need to spend more time with the people explaining instead of just appearing for several hours and expecting people to enlist. I asked him what he thought of the recruiting techniques that Gustavo explained to me.

'There is one aspect that is good about it, and that is that there are a number of kids that may want to go with the *compas* but are afraid that their families will be pointed out by the 'ears' and killed. Going as if they are being forced to makes everything all right. Their parents can say "the *compas* took them."

If the foreign press doesn't like it to hell with them, they're not fighting this war. . .'

I asked him how the people reacted to the taking of the Cerrón Grande Dam. He said very differently from the way they reacted to other big battles. The taking of Paraíso, in 1983, represented a major military triumph and the beginning of a new stage in the war, but it and other battles did not connect with the people. The taking of the dam, as a statement in defense of the strikers, made the people realize that the FMLN and the workers are together.

Andrés studied two years in the university. During his first year his family said, 'If you want to have a family you can't join the guerrillas.' He left home, finished his second year and came to the mountains. There is a lot he wants to study in the political field. In the military, he said, there is only so much to learn then it's just a matter of tactics and strategies. He is being moved back into the military, and feels that the organization does not understand him, or that he was doing something wrong but doesn't know what.

I have just received a note from Chevo telling me that, because of enemy movement in the area, I am to pick up all my stuff and meet so-and-so down the mountain, at such a time, and go to María's. We've had these scares before, and I don't feel anything in the air, and I don't want to go, but an order is an order, and so so-and-so carried my camera bag, and off we went. Here at María's they are preparing for a *guinda*. With the possibility of a *guinda*, everybody reminisces about their last one and each story is quite depressing.

Well, just as I thought, there is no *guinda*, but I must stay a couple more days till the area is completely secure. The Belloso battalion (an elite unit but not as elite as the Atlacatl) left La Dos after suffering 42 casualties. Recently, after the Atlacatl suffered 64 casualties down in Cabañas, morale went down because that was the first time an elite unit had been hit so hard. And now with 42 I guess they decided to take a rest. Between the elite and the general troops (called *Cazadores*) the government forces have suffered 1,300 casualties in the last two months.

Staying with María is quite a trip. We also eat well (within the limitations) since she loves to cook. Last night after dinner those of us who smoked pulled out our cigarettes and lit up. Her husband, José, was one of us.

'José smokes too much. You know, he has smoked cows, cows!' María said.

To myself I thought: What does she mean by cows? Amount? Since cows are enormous? Then I realized: of course, she means money; cows represent money. She was referring to the amount of money spent on this habit.

'Aside from smoking all these cows', she went on, 'it's not something that we share. He does it all alone.'

I think she's wonderful.

Later on they were talking about organizing people. María said that the *compas* meet with the women in the hamlets and explain how important it is for them to get organized, that it will strengthen the party, etc. 'That's not what you say to them', said María, 'You say, organize yourselves around building a chicken coop and then you can eat an egg a day. One egg a day, that's enough to organize anyone!'

Well, the state of emergency is over and I can go back to my house. According to one of the national radios the Belloso was planning something big here. But they left. A *compa* passing through said that a captain of the battalion was preparing to take the Montañona – a strategic mountain that must always be taken if there is an invasion around here – and stopped a peasant coming down it, asking if there were any guerrillas up there and how many? The peasant said he didn't know, but five horses laden with sacks of corn and beans had been going up everyday. The captain did some calculations and decided not to take the Montañona.

Good morning with nine bombs. That's how many I've counted so far. Don't know where they are bombing but I can see the smoke and feel the ground rumble. The last bombing I watched was not in Los Amates but in Jicarito. Most of the houses were destroyed, eight dead and six injured. The shrapnel from these bombs can cut you in half or decapitate you. They explode just before they hit the ground – daisy cutters I believe they're called. Fortunately it was 10:00 hrs so most people were out working in the fields, if not more would have died. Today is Sunday and it's 07:00 hrs. Just what do they think they're doing? Trying to kill people, what else?

Andrés told me about one particularly horrible bombing he lived through. He was walking through the smoke right after it fell and saw a little girl crawling without legs, a man, his whole back ripped open, crawling towards a little boy all covered in blood, a woman many months pregnant with her belly cut open and the baby lying blown out near by.

Oh God, it goes on and on. I would guess all this makes joining the FMLN a lot easier. How much of this can you take before you decide to fight back? Especially now that the FMLN has power, has an army and territory. I should think that my own reaction to my first bombing attack is the same for most: first fear, then rage.

It was a beautiful day but the bombs ruined it.

Chevo came by to talk to me. Bad news. I ain't going nowhere for the moment. He had three things to propose: (1) that I get my film developed in a little town so that it won't go bad and will be easier to take out (2) that I organize my material so that it can be sent back to the US; and (3) once that is done, and he wants me to do it at *Propa* because nobody likes me staying alone in this house, that I start another project, get involved in something else.

My answer to 1 was no, and to 2 and 3 yes. But in order to organize my material I have to write, which means I will not go to *Propa* because I can't think in that mess, which means I need coffee, soap, candles, typewriter and paper. He said OK.

So last night I got soap for clothes and body, candles and cigarettes. Coffee, the messenger said, Chevo couldn't get, but he would. So goodnight folks, I now have a candle to see the bats with.

OK, here we are Taina, What to do? Transcribe last interview, organize film and describe contents. Maybe start with a short article on the Christians for Maryknoll. How can I concentrate with all of these planes?

The final toll of the town bombed the other day: eleven bombs, seven dead, five injured, eleven houses and part of the corn fields destroyed. A thirteen-year old boy told how when he heard the planes coming he ran out of the house but his father stayed. A bomb fell right on the house. Bits of trees, earth and shrapnel went flying by him but he was not hurt. When it was over he watched as others dug up bits and pieces of his father, put him in a container and buried him. What does that child think today?

Now that the rainy season has begun the vegetation around here grows inches overnight. Between it and the spider webs I'm going to need a machete to get to the outhouse. Literally, the weeds are taller than me and a week ago they were not.

My problem right now is paper. How can I write without paper? I want to translate the interview with Tilo and with the delegates. But on what? My pen is going to run out soon. This using a bic pen to the very last drop is another way of living. The one I have now has a section of ink caught up at the other end – that's pages and pages of writing that I can't use.

My spirits are going down again. It's the nights all by myself with the insects, the bats, the darkness and nothing to do but sleep, and I can't sleep. I don't like the night. I can't get depressed. I can't. Is this ever going to end? Am I ever going to get out of here? Are my family and friends worried? Oh God, I'm tired of being a sponge. People here call me a journalist but I'm not a journalist. I'm a sponge walking around absorbing other people's lives, stories, feelings, experiences. There is no me. I don't seem to exist here. There is only them. And I think about the people I love out there, and then I think that I have no right to think about them because here are a people suffering, dying, fighting – but I matter and they matter and we all matter, each one of us with all of what we are, what makes us individuals, and then all together. A little of me and everyone, a little of you and everyone, a little of us and everyone. Otherwise there wouldn't be everyone. I feel so sad. . .

Well, here we are folks, another day in beautiful Chalatenango. *Buenos días camaradas*.

Some combatants just dropped by for a rest and a drink of water. I was writing at my desk when one of them came over, watched me and then said, 'We've met before. Do you remember me?' It turned out we had trekked across

Guazapa together with Negro Dulce when we first came in. Guerri. Of course I remember him. He was all smiles, was in the K-97, had fought in Cerrón Grande where he got his first battle scars, and he was having a great time.

He said that after we separated in El Sitio (other side of lake), he was taken to *Propa* (another *Propa*) because they wanted him to work there as he is well educated. But he said no, he wanted to be a combatant. Then there was a *guinda* and he was in Tehutla and met some *compas* who said: 'Come on with us.' Guerri said, 'Yeah! Let's go!' And here he is with the K-93.

During our walk together in Guazapa Guerri had told me that when he was 12 years old the National Guard killed his brother in San Salvador, and he had sworn to himself that when he turned 16 he would join the guerrillas. He had just turned 16.

We talked about the trek. I asked him if he remembered when Negro Dulce told him to carry my camera bag he didn't want to and Negro Dulce ordered him to carry it.

'Yes, yes! I really admired you. Your first long walk with all that stuff and me, I'm a man and have more resistance, and I could hardly manage it. And there you were carrying it when it was your turn and keeping up with the rest of us.'

He told a friend later how the *compas* kept saying, 'Oh, just one more little mountain and we'll be there.'

'Bullshit!' he said, 'There were ten more of them. Hours we walked! No?'

Bad news. Esteban said that what they were planning is not secure enough right now so they have decided to make me a passport. If the situation changes I won't need to use it, if it doesn't then I can get out with the passport. Jesus! Make me a passport? Are you kidding? No, Esteban said, they are not kidding. He asked if I had a picture of myself – which I happened to have. He apologized for all the delay. What can I say? He then told me that he did not like the idea of my staying alone in that house. I explained why I wanted to stay and he said OK. He wanted to know what I would like to get involved in when I finish what I'm doing. I told him some of my thoughts. Fine. Another apology. It's all right man, I understand, this is a war. What is there to fucking say?

I am considering getting my feet fixed in San Juan where Victoria works. Victoria is a German doctor working at Post 8. It's a hospital for long-term injuries and physical therapy. She herself is a bone specialist.

She, Karla and Claudia spent the night last night and during our conversation I showed her my feet.

'Oh God! You must feel a lot of pain when you walk.'

Yes, yes, at least someone understands what it feels like! She told me to go to her place, she'll cut them out and a week later my feet will be like new. Oh, yes, I'm going!

Great! New feet! Maybe next week. I must finish this article first.

When I hear war stories I want to be there, when I hear learning stories there, too, I want to be. So I have to finish the article, get my feet fixed, and while the X-21 is on R&R, I'll spend some time with the masses and then go off with them.

I've not been able to write all afternoon. Here comes the rain again. I feel like going to the movies or sitting in an outdoor cafe drinking a beer or something – anything other than this. I have a great title, a great ending, most of the meat but I can't get the beginning of this article. Too much that I want to say. Douglas walked by this morning and yelled out, 'You are going to write great things Taina! I feel it.' Yeah, Douglas, I'm up to 14 different butterflies – almost inhaled one this morning. The latest ones are dancing pairs – black and red. There is no bridge between butterflies and Christians. Hell. Another future butterfly – they are all over the place, covered in white fluff, all over me, my papers. If they all make it I'm not going to be able to see past all the butterflies. Better than a movie, I suppose.

The camouflage in this world! It's one great violent universe! I can't stand it! And why shouldn't these people fight for a better life? Why not? Why shouldn't they kill if it will change a system that has treated them like animals, like beasts of burden, to one that will treat them like human beings? How much more of this are they supposed to take? This country is so full of violence and death, and has been for a hell of a long time. And Americans spend millions of dollars just so they can watch violence and death in movie theaters and on television. Why do they like watching it so much?

I have no paper and no typewriter, so I can't write. I guess I'll slowly make my way to San Juan and get my feet fixed. I'll go to Tamarindo and find someone who can take me there. I've sent a note to Esteban telling him where I'm going and why. Either I get out or get in but I refuse to be 'awaiting' anymore.

I took all of my equipment, film and the little else I have and don't want to carry down to Sonia's for safekeeping while I'm gone. When I handed them over to her I said, 'Sonia, I'm giving you all of my work. You must guard it with your life!' Then, jokingly, I said, 'If there's an invasion don't you dare leave it behind.'

I'm in Tamarindo. It's Tuesday morning, 06:00 hrs, and mortars are falling all around us. An hour later they stop and I'm told that a 24-day old baby has been badly injured and is at the hospital. I go over there and photograph her. She's a mess. As I photograph her I think that she's just a doll and it's only stuffing that I see. There's no way she will survive. Meanwhile, there are a couple of 'push&pulls' (O-2A spotter planes) flying around. Definitely a lot of activity in the air and around us.

There is a quick funeral for the child. No one seems to know what's happening. I go back to the house where I had spent the night. There is no one around. I do a little writing and by noon I can clearly hear the sounds of battle just over the other side of the mountain. Someone comes rushing by and says that the enemy is in Las Flores (about a 20-minute walk from here).

I pack my knapsack and walk though town. It looks deserted. I bump into Tita with another person, looking very anxious, on their way back to the house to get their stuff. Then I see Reyes and he tells me that this is an invasion, that the people have gone down there, in that direction, and I should get my ass over there. One 'push&pull' is circling low over the town and the guns are getting closer.

OK, this is getting serious. Something inside of me says, you are not going to go with those people, they are totally disorganized and that could be dangerous. I decide to go to María's, about one and half hour's walk from here. That means that I've got to get up to the mountain pass, but with the 'push&pull' circling so low I decide to go down via the corn fields, for cover, and then figure a way up to the pass from there. As I crawl up the side of the mountain I think, Jesus Christ! My first invasion and I'm all alone. But it's all right because I know where I'm going and I'm not with that group of 300 frightened people and kids.

I get to the pass and there are Pedro Guerra and Camila from the RN[17] (I'd had coffee with them before the mortars). I'm glad to see them. They tell me that Chacho is around so I feel good – if Chacho is around everything's cool. Pedro has a huge radio that can intercept enemy radio conversation. We hear them ask for an A-37 to bomb Tamarindo and, specifically, the hospital. I decide I'll hang around and shoot the bombing. Chacho appears and we wait for the plane. First they can't find one, and then when they do, we hear them say not to bomb because their troops are too close.

Chacho tells us to go to María's. Do I know the way? Because Pedro and Camila don't know the territory here. Chacho is going to stay with some militias to get more info and will meet us at María's. I think it's quite bizarre that I, a foreigner, am leading a *comandante* and his *compa*/bodyguard through the mountains of El Salvador during an invasion. When we're almost at María's, Andrecito appears and takes Pedro and Camila with him.

There's a large group of people hanging around at María's. Chevo is here, all of *Propa*, all of María's people, and everyone is preparing for a *guinda*. They've been preparing all afternoon and I was just on my way to get my feet fixed.

María is obviously the leader. She passes out one-pound bags of sugar to various people and divides us into subgroups for better organization. I am put behind Julio in the line. She tells us that the Atlacatl has invaded the zone, they've taken Tamarindo, they are over there, and over there, and we are going to go over there and then over there. I don't know where there is but it doesn't matter and I don't know that I like being on a *guinda* with mostly civilians – no radios, few weapons – it ain't the X-21.

Chacho and his boys arrive. There are 45 of us: a one-and-a-half-year old baby, seven other children between the ages of four and ten, two very old people, and the rest of us in between. At 21:00 hrs we get into our positions and step off into the night.

We walk. It rains. The path is rugged and covered with stones and mud. At one point the rain is so bad and the night so dark that we have to hold on to each other's knapsacks so as not to get lost or separated from the group. We move silently up and down mountains, cross knee-high rivers with our boots on, and it rains and rains.

At 03:00 hrs we get to the Sumpul river. Dangling high above is a dilapidated hanging bridge suspended by thin cables wound around trees on either side, only the cable on the right is not as tight as the one on the left, the wooden boards on which you step here and there leave huge holes of blackness and the roar of the river below. It's a bitch and it's night and we have babies and children that have to be carried over and everybody is scared to death and it takes hours to cross. It's almost dawn by the time everybody has crossed. We walk another hour and get to a little deserted hamlet. María tells us to rest.

This hamlet is in an area of Chalate called Chichilco, where María was born and raised. She knows the territory. Good. Chevo and Gregorio, a newly arrived *compa* from the capital here for a visit, go back to the bridge to look for Chacho who stayed behind waiting for the masses from Tamarindo. Everyone is extremely frightened but they try to relax. I'm not, because this is my first invasion and I don't hear anything. It's a lovely sunny day so I pull out my hammock, take off my soaking wet jeans, socks and boots and try to sleep.

Suddenly an A-37 comes screeching over our heads and bombs the area. It doesn't last long. My group has jumped into the bushes away from the houses and stays there. I pack my hammock, check that they haven't left me, sit on the ground and put my shrivelled-up feet (from being wet inside boots and walking all night) and boots in the sun to dry.

Well, there I am, watching the steam rising from by boots when bang, bang, bang! bullets flying all over the place. I jump into my socks, into my boots, grab my knapsack and run off with everybody else. María yells at us to stay together and leads us running while the bullets fly behind our backs.

Up and down we go, crawling most of the time. Hours go by. We don't hear any more guns but we know that the enemy is somewhere nearby. We go up the side of another mountain, covered in tall grass, and suddenly we hear helicopters and a hell of a lot of shooting. This is getting pretty hairy. We can see the helicopters, they're flying in a circle, they're getting closer and we're sitting in the grass. The whole side of the mountain is covered in grass. What the hell are we going to do?

I look at the faces around me: they look like trapped animals, and I feel like one, and I think, Jesus Christ, we may die here. María sends word to us to follow her, hunched over as low as possible. We move. We get to a low rock wall, grass everywhere and nowhere to hide. María tells us to sit close to the wall and not to move. We sit. I can hear people screaming, machine-guns, grenades and the helicopters circling and circling.

I panic and decide that this is where I'm going to die. Then I tell myself to calm down, that if I'm going to die, then I'm going to die and since there is nothing I can do about it, cool it, Taina. I calm down. The helicopters get closer and I am suddenly filled with rage. I can't believe that these goddamn soldiers are mowing down unarmed people. Killing people from helicopters. It infuriates me, and for the first time in my life I want a gun, because I can't stand the thought of these cowards killing me and others without a fight. No way man. Whatever the horrors of war, this is not allowed. You can't shoot defenseless adults and children. You can't do it. It's not right. And we sit and listen to the screams and we know that time is not on our side.

Off on the horizon we see big black clouds moving in our direction. We start whispering madly, 'Come, come clouds, please rain!' Someone next to me is praying to God to send the rain to us. Because we know that helicopters won't fly in rain storms. And the clouds come and it thunders, and we are all chanting, 'Rain, rain, rain.' The sky turns black and a torrential rain falls. The helicopters go, the guns stop. Julio and I begin to kiss the raindrops, everyone is giggling hysterically as the rain pours down on us. María whispers, 'OK, everybody move fast, low to the ground!' We go, slithering and crawling, through the wet grass like snakes. Several hours later, already into the night, we get to some woods and María tells us to rest. We've almost been killed, we're soaking wet, we've not eaten since yesterday, it's pouring rain and we lie down in the rain and sleep.

Next morning we walk several hours, find a river covered in thick vegetation and sit in the damp undergrowth for the rest of the day. Our subgroup – Julio and a few others from *Propa* and I – ration out a handful of sugar three times a day. We listen to the radio, can't get the Farabundo or the Venceremos stations,[18] and some national station says that there are 2,000 soldiers in Chalate, and several other thousands in Usulután, Morazán and Guazapa. At least it's national, so the troops are dispersed. María sends out scouts. We hear shooting but not too near. Everyone is sitting on their plastic drying out their shrivelled-up feet. We move out at night, get to a pleasant hill, the stars are out, no rain and we sleep.

I woke up in the morning to discover that most of my poncho was gone. I must have spilled some sugar on it just before sleeping and the ants ate it while I slept. I can't believe it! Now what do I do when it rains?

It's my fourth day without eating, third day for everybody else. Who knows when this will end. I don't hear anything. As far as I'm concerned there is nothing happening around here. Julio says that usually after the third day the enemy gets exhausted and starts to leave.

We are near the Honduran border, and if things should get worse we'll go to Honduras. We still have no information. We don't know who the Atlacatl was shooting at the other day. Was it the folks from Tamarindo? Who knows. Hell, it's been interesting, but fuck wars.

I suppose we'll spend the day here. What we need is information: where are the troops; are we hiding for nothing? María has sent two *compas* to Honduras to see about getting some food. OK, food I can definitely think about.

We ate today! The two *compas* came back from Honduras with tortillas, bread and cheese. The Hondurans in the town they went to stayed up all night making us food. Talk about solidarity.

We got a note from Chevo. He's all right. It was the folks from Tamarindo who were caught crossing the river the other day. Gregorio, the visiting *compa*, was killed and Tita has been captured. It's a mess. The masses are dispersed. Chevo is with a group about as large as ours, all women and children. He will stay with them and wants us to await further notice. He has a radio and is trying to get in touch with the FPL military.

Well, we're still here. Unnecessarily, as far as I'm concerned. Nobody wants to spend the night in this place again. It was the worst night possible. Julio and I shared his and my bitsy plastic and it rained and we got soaked, and pain all over my body because of the hard ground. It was terrible. Nobody slept. María and her daughter woke up this morning and their skin was all shrivelled up from the water.

Chevo came by and gave more details. The large group from Tamarindo fell asleep walking so they only arrived at the bridge at dawn. The government forces discovered them and started shooting. The column broke up. They dispersed all around where we were resting and then a group was discovered by the enemy. That's when they brought in the helicopters. Slaughter from the helicopters, pure slaughter. We were saved by the rain – nothing more, nothing less. It's all very sickening. All I ask is that my notebooks and photos are safe so that I can do something to stop this.

We came down into a valley late afternoon yesterday and hid in a deserted farm compound. First night that we've slept without getting wet. What a pleasure. This compound has a lovely waterfall where we all bathed and washed some things. We spent the rest of the morning sitting in the sun and drying out. Scouts came back and said things look calm. We still don't know anything.

Suddenly fighting breaks out but not that near and María screams at us to get our things and get the hell out. Into the river everybody hysterically goes. Hunted animals scrambling up a river. Some are so panicked that they fall into it. I can't believe the hysteria and the fear. Everybody is getting wet and covered with mud after spending the whole morning bathing, washing and drying. It's all getting to be slightly ridiculous. In the beginning there was real danger but now – I don't feel it. So there is another battle but we are not the target. So they are obviously fighting the *compas* and they have planes and helicopters and mortars, but it's not with us, damn it.

I almost don't go up the river. I can't believe they're doing what they're doing, and I think that eventually they'll calm down and come back. Then I am told to get my ass up the river, so calmly and coolly I move up – damned if I'm going to get wet again for no bloody reason.

When I arrive to where they are huddling under some trees I am reprimanded for my slowness and told that I will be put up ahead in the column so that won't happen again. I want to say, 'Fuck you folks' but I keep my mouth shut. It's not my war, it's not my country, it's my first *guinda*, but I'll be damned if I'm going to get hysterical over nothing. These people are freaked out.

Julio has turned into a very ugly person on this *guinda*. The whole dynamics of this group is overwhelmingly awful, selfish and stupid. I can't stand it or them.

Oh Christ, we're still doing this. Two nights ago we slept in the tall prickly grass – at least it didn't rain. Then we moved to a plot of dried out *maizillo* stalks. We sit here all day and all night and it rains and rains. It's too ridiculous. I can't stand these people, this country, this war. I've had it – I want out, out, no more.

It's the selfishness that's destroying me. Worse now than when I first entered the front because we are in a *guinda*. A number of people in this group packed rice, tortillas, potatoes, salt, candy, crackers, etc., when they knew there was going to be a *guinda*. In the ensuing days they munched on their personal cache in front of anybody who was around. Some of us, in groups, had sugar. A few had absolutely nothing because they were not part of a group. I had nothing because I did not prepare for a *guinda*, neither would I have thought of taking food, but I was part of the film *mara* so I got my ration of sugar those first three days.

On the third day when that first wave of danger was over Julio came up to me and said that someone was going to a little town to buy. Didn't I want to buy some bread? I said, sure, I'll contribute, I'll buy bread. How about eight loaves? He thought that was great and I gave him some money and he went to order it. Well, I thought we were going to put all the money together and buy for the whole group. Those who had money would buy and those who didn't would participate. I figured this one had to be communal as we had almost died together, and been through one hell of a three-day horror show. But when the stuff came Julio brought the bread and said to put it in my knapsack.

I realized that there wasn't going to be any sharing. I didn't want eight loaves (these were very small loaves) just for myself so I gave half of them away. While I still had some Julio became my best buddy as he wanted bread. Everybody was groveling for a handout. When my bread ran out I decided no more. I will buy cigarettes but I will not eat if someone else does not. The unsharing in the midst of a *guinda* has devastated me. I am horrified by it.

When we all got food from Honduras that was good. Then it was back to yours and mine. Several more times a *compa* went off to buy for those with money. The look on the faces of those without when the *compa* handed out the individual orders was just too hungry. How can anybody eat in front of somebody else who is starving? Especially under these conditions? No. I cannot accept this.

Now that we are in the eighth day of this *guinda*, María has decided (she who had the biggest personal cache in the group) that there will no longer be any individual food – all food will be collective, not cigarettes.

It's been ten days. We are still huddled in the vegetation. After each rainy night I take myself, my cover and my camera to a spot in the sun and dry us out. If a plane goes by, even the commercial one, everybody panics. I don't understand this irrational fear. It's been ten days, surely, the Atlacatl has gone. But they continue to huddle in fear and I in solitude. I will not relate to these people, they have broken my heart. They really have.

We were liberated today. Three militias spent all day looking for us – we were that well hidden. It's over, the invasion is over. It was over the day before yesterday. Everybody went yelling and laughing down the mountain and then we bought a pig, collectively, in a little town. I went for a walk while they were cooking it. When I got back there was a big fight about collective and individual food. I don't understand why it wasn't worked out during the first few days of the *guinda*. Now that it's over it seems a little late and absurd to me. To hell with it, they can do what they want. I don't care.

September

The cost of the invasion: 11 *compa* casualties, 55 civilians killed and 50 captured. Houses and crops were hardly damaged. The massacre occurred because, unknowingly, we walked towards the mountain that the enemy had taken to assure the exit of their troops. They were not expecting us nor we them. When they saw the masses crossing the bridge they attacked. Then they knew there were people around so they went hunting for us. That's when Gregorio was killed, when they were advancing in the direction of the little town we were resting in. They were very close. And there I was sleeping in my hammock with my jeans off and then sunbathing my feet.

We then went up and around the mountain. The masses stayed down and went around slowly. As the Atlacatl moved on, in the afternoon, they caught up with the masses and killed some of them – that's when we were almost caught. The next day when we were sitting by the river and heard the rapid firing it was also the Atlacatl having discovered another group hiding. That's when Tita was captured.

When I got back to Cordoncillo I found that my house was a total wreck. Many people must have passed through there during the invasion. The water was cut off, the place was upside down and filthy. I have decided to go stay down at Sonia's until I can get into contact with Esteban and figure out what the hell I do next with my life.

All of my equipment and film are safe. When Sonia was told to prepare for a *guinda* she buried them with all of the other supplies.

Everyone is exhausted by the *guinda*. Sonia had a terrible time. She was with four others and they had no idea where they were, no food, no coordination, and the enemy always around. Must have been terrible.

The rain never stops, it only gets worse. How can the earth take any more water? I am reaching a point where I can't stand to see any more water, any more mud.

The bottom of my hammock busted last night. I don't know if it can be mended this time. Quite honestly I've had it. My whole being is sad and damp.

Esteban sent a note saying that he's glad I'm well and safe. He is going away for a while and all he knows is that my document is being made but he doesn't know when it will arrive. Douglas is now responsible for me and will arrange my exit should the passport appear or the other alternative be secured while he is gone. So, by the way he wrote, it seems that I am 'awaiting' once again. What the hell am I supposed to think? Am I staying or leaving? And if I'm leaving, how? A false passport? I think Scarlett O'Hara had the right attitude: I won't think about it today, I'll think about it tomorrow, or something like that. Hell. . .

Marga, a Spanish doctor, came by and was very happy to see me. Rumor had it, throughout the *guinda*, that I was captured and Tita dead, then, it turned out, that I was dead and Tita captured.

During the first two years of the war the *compas* protected the masses during invasions, which meant they couldn't attack the enemy. These days the *compas* deal with the enemy and the masses are supposed to take care of themselves. The idea being that they should be better organized now, should have built their own underground shelters, should be better able to cope. A number of people did not go running off because they hid in their shelters. Once the enemy passed through they were back to living somewhat normally, unlike the masses from Tamarindo and elsewhere who wore themselves out and got themselves killed. It's ironic that it was the people from Tamarindo who got hit the worst, as that is the center of Popular Power; the leaders were totally out of control and the area in chaos.

A lot of it has to do with the fact that this zone has not had a major invasion since last year and so the masses got too relaxed, too sloppy. Each hamlet is supposed to have its own system of nightwatch and territorial militias. What seems to have happened, on the night of the 27th, is that the ones on duty were sleeping and when they woke up in the morning there was the Atlacatl. They had moved into the zone during the night. Something the enemy has rarely done. As they say, never underestimate the enemy and never overestimate yourself.

The *guinda* stories continue and the picture becomes clearer and more incomprehensible on the part of the enemy. It seems that the Atlacatl swept through the zone very defensively, did not use the roads or paths because they were afraid they were mined. They always chose the highest areas and didn't go down. When they left ten days later, through Patanera and beyond, the people who saw them go said they were exhausted and haggard – this is the elite of the elite.

The X-21 had just arrived, the day before, for R&R and were hanging around without boots and without batteries for their radios. By chance they sent out two *compas* to take a look around 20 minutes before the Atlacatl arrived and off they went, barefoot and without communication. Later on, there was a total lack of coordination between them and the K-23 – when they finally had batteries they didn't have the codes for Chalate.

The hospitals were also totally disorganized. The one in San Juan heard about the invasion when the Atlacatl was moving in their direction but luckily they evacuated all the injured before it arrived.

All in all, it was a total mess and the consequences of this mess were: 16 *compa* casualties, 50 massacred, 57 captured, one hospital destroyed and one mined, and little damage throughout the zone. Crazy. I'm beginning to believe in the 'luck of the guerrilla'.

Chacho came by. We gave each other big hugs because we thought the other dead. Chacho was told that my body had been seen lying on the ground. He and his small group spent the *guinda* in style: they slept in empty houses, sent out scouts all the time, ate three times a day, had a radio but not the updated codes (radio communication is done with numbers and those numbers change every other week). He said that, at one point, they went looking for us to tell us it was just about over but. . . yeah, I know. The *compas* from the *Comité* and the *Chile* joke about how when the invasion was over, María's group was still hiding and were so well hidden that it took two days for the militias to find them. Ha ha ha.

This *guinda* has broken me. The paranoia and the selfishness and the rain created an enormous despair in me. Fear can make people very ugly. The collective psychosis of the hunted: every bullet, every combat, every plane, every mortar, every bomb was directed personally at them. Crazy.

This despair has not left me now that I am back. When it rains it is there, when these people talk about their *guinda* for the hundredth time it is there, when I think of my project it is there. I am in a state of despair, and have been for over two weeks. Seven months I've been alone, with no identity in this country. I've got to get out of here so help me God. I've given just about all, much more than I could afford to. I am physically and emotionally broken.

Someone just stole my brand new blue underpants that I had saved for reserve. Now I have only one pair – great – thanks a lot.

I helped Soila make soap, the kind I've been using for the last several months: a dark brown ball of gook that doesn't dry out the skin or scalp. It's quite a process. They gather nuts from a certain tree, break open the very hard shell, put the pits in a big cauldron with water and ashes and let it cook all week, stirring and stirring it. Eventually it looks like bubbling chocolate.

Actually, doing anything in these mountains is a time-consuming process. Eating is a daily chore. Looking for firewood, cooking and grinding the corn, making tortillas, eating them, and starting all over again. Plus planting the stuff and picking each grain off the ear. Surviving takes all day. I spent most of yesterday toasting and grinding my coffee. As Sonia and I took turns grinding I said, 'I think I read somewhere that they invented electricity some years ago, no?'

Ten combatants from the X-21 are hanging around and sleeping here at the store. One group is waiting for a shipment of boots – everybody's getting boots now – and the other for their M-60 to be fixed. They talk about fighting and giggle all the time while their radio plays rock and roll. The big, bad, ugly guerrillas. I doubt that they think of themselves in romantic terms. It's possible to want to idealize them and their motives, but I think their greatness is in their simplicity and, in a way, their lack of 'ideology'. They're kids and they're playing very hard. Only I don't want to play anymore.

Is it possible for those outside to understand that people can fight without having an ideology? I don't know that it takes a political ideology or intellectual reasoning to choose a side, to understand that poverty is not desirable, or that the repressive apparatus used to protect a minority's wealth is just. For us in the First World perhaps it is difficult to understand motivation without a political/intellectual analysis. But I think that their motivation comes from reacting to a violent existence. We can theorize about the positions we take in life, but they don't have the luxury to do so, nor the education.

In a way I think it's good that I've spent more time here than I expected to, because I have lived more and perhaps understood more. I don't know what the middle class thinks or the working class, but the peasants, them I know something about, even if I can't relate to them, even if our worlds are too far apart.

It rained and rained last night. My soul is flooded with solitude. I try not to think too much about the fact that a batch of passports is arriving soon, or to hope that they will come up with a better idea. The days go by and the mud curls around my brain. Being with Sonia and her group is completely boring. Small itsybitsy worlds that I don't want any part of. Too much boredom with no relief, and I worry about the lack of stimulation for the kids. I spoke to Sonia about that and she had no idea what I was talking about. No one is stimulated here and they don't care – war is the stimulant and that's it.

I went to J-15, a military medical base, that is off-limits for most people. I've been here so long that no one found it inappropriate that I appeared in a place that I was not allowed in four months ago. I showed a doctor the hard lumps in my breasts and explained that I had not menstruated the seven months that I've been here. She said they were not attached, probably just glands, but she wanted a second opinion and told me to go over and see Marga. Marga checked them and confirmed what the other doctor said. They can order a drug from the capital that will make my period come, but since I'm about to leave any day now, why not wait until I get out? OK with me.

Marga is working in public health these days and goes around to all the different hamlets, listens to people's ailments and gives advice and/or medicine depending on availability. When I found her she was sitting at a table under a tree and a line of people were waiting to talk to her. A woman sat down to consult with her. She had gray, straggly hair, most teeth were missing, an old haggard face and body with a distended stomach that had birthed many a child. Marga asked her how old she was and she said 36. She was my age! She looked 30 years older. No wonder when I mention my age most people think I'm making it up. There is no justification for this amount of poverty, none.

The minutes go through the days here covered in mud and time oozes by as the rain seeps into the earth. Everything is soaked and soggy and we breathe water. The black clouds come and go, and another day ends and another wet, long night is about to begin. And we sleep through the wet and the darkness, and when the light finally penetrates through the green, it's another day with more rain and mud. We are completely caught by nature and a war that move with the same rhythm. How much more water and how much more blood can this earth absorb?

All paths become rivers and the bones become like stones, all washed clean by the water as it flows through the rib cage, around the cranium, over the hand holding onto a rock with bits of flesh still on the fingertips, all white and clean and wet. We continue along the path muddying the water as we plod on. The rain begins again, the bones are left behind. How long will that hand hold that rock? But it doesn't really matter if it keeps on holding or finally lets go. Does it?

I have mud instead of blood in my veins but I did photograph the human pebbles in the stream we slush through. Who were they? Three adults and a child by the size of the craniums. Their bones are their identity. They were people eleven days ago, but that was such a long time ago.

The invasion is finally over, the enemy has left, we are going back to where we live and the bones and the memories are left behind. Slushing through the muddy waters it doesn't matter anymore, nothing matters because we are now free and human again and not animals. Yes, the invasion is over and we're human again – those of us who were lucky.

And it keeps on raining and the mud slides down the mountain and another week has ended, or maybe it's another month. I have a waterproof electronic watch so I know, but it doesn't really matter what day it is or what month, it doesn't really matter what time it is. It is day, it is night, it is life, it is war in El Salvador.

It rained all night and parts of the house fell in while we slept. Now the morning is fogged and gloomy. Randu came by to have his M-60 fixed. He asked me what my status was and I explained.

'But you don't want to go yet anyway, do you?' He said. 'All kinds of interesting things are going to happen in October. You don't want to miss them, do you?'

Yeah, right. People don't seem to understand or to be aware of the fact that there is another world out there and that I have something to do with it, and that maybe I've had enough of theirs. But why should they be aware of this? There is only one world – theirs.

This war is so Salvadoran that at times I feel imprisoned by its Salvadoranness, feel that I'm suffocating with a people that only know their own poverty, their own hunger, their own struggle to survive, and now their own war.

And people shit or pee right around the house because to go further would require more energy. They blow their noses in their hands or onto the floor and wipe their hands on the back of a bench, wall or rail, and they spit – they are forever spitting – and the kids crawl through it all sucking their fingers, their growth stunted by all the parasites, by all the poverty. And they never had toys or books or games or youth. They don't know how to play, how to interact, to discover or to ask. And then, still kids, they start having babies and the cycle repeats itself, generation after generation. And I say this war is being fought so that these people can have toys and books and schools and, most of all, so that they can be children and grow as healthy children do, instead of being old and sick and worn out by the age of 30.

Well, here we are waiting for orders to *guindiar*. Yesterday all store materiel was carted off to underground places. I refused to believe in another invasion so I kept my stuff out. By this morning I realized I needed to be ready to run, so I talked to Sonia.

'It's too late', she said, 'to store your equipment underground because all the places have been sealed and camouflaged. I told you to give it to me yesterday.'

'Yes, I know, but what am I to do?'

'Wrap the bag and whatever else you don't want to take in this plastic and I'll go throw it in the bushes where no one will find it.'

'You're going to throw my work in the bushes? What about the rain and the sun and the soldiers?'

'Taina, I told you yesterday to give it to me. You didn't. This is the best I can do. Wrap it up and give it to me.'

I did and watched as she disappeared with my work in her arms up the side of the mountain.

It is exactly one month since the Atlacatl invaded. They told the population of La Laguna that they would be back in a month – and here they are. Needless to say, I don't feel very excited about any of this. It's a beautiful day, blue sky, and the planes have come and bombed all around, mortars have fallen, even rockets. We are now lying on the ground, resting, waiting for orders.

The Atlacatl is in several places but as of this morning they have not advanced.

At 13:00 hrs we finally receive orders to move up to the command post. We join around 200 other *compas*; Lieutenant Jacinto, commander of this battalion, tells us that the Atlacatl has taken the Montañona. The *compas* are fighting them now. While they fight we are going to go around the base of the mountain and then over there.

'Since it is daylight and the enemy can see us everyone must camouflage themselves. The column will move at a fast pace and there will be 15 meters between each person. No one closes the space. OK, let's get moving.'

Covered in leaves and keeping close to any vegetation we can find, we go down the mountain and over there. We can hear the battle in the Montañona. At one point it seems they have discovered the column because we get some heavy mortaring. We keep on walking. Late evening we stop near some hamlet and are told that we will spend the night here. It's all rocks and no one can sleep. It's bloody cold but it doesn't rain, only our feet are soaking wet from the rivers we had to cross. A group from the X-21 comes through to pick up more ammo. Then we are told that the enemy is coming down the Montañona so at 05:00 hrs we move out.

It sure is different *guindiando* with armed *compas* and radios. Even if this group is not a fighting battalion it is still a battalion. As we pass through certain areas there are *compas* already there and on the watch. I wonder where the masses have run off to this time; where María's group and *Propa* are hiding. I'm glad I'm not with them. There isn't any collective neurosis here. Sometimes with the planes bombing and the helicopters flying and the sounds of battle not too far and not too near, a few get nervous and scream 'Advance, advance!' Which is a little difficult as the head of the column is way the hell up front. But other than that it's been pretty cool. A lot of walking though. My feet are killing me and Sonia's cook is carrying her three-year old kid on her shoulders on top of her knapsack.

We have been hanging around a river all morning and at 16:00 hrs we are given the order to move up the mountain to form the column. We are already two-thirds of the way up. As we get to the top firing breaks out and we are given the order to go down the mountain. There is total panic, total. We go flying down the river on our asses in chaos and fear. Just about everybody has an M-16 over their shoulders as they scurry down the river, and I ask myself what the hell are we running for, in complete disorder and panic and perhaps getting ourselves killed in the process, if everyone is armed. How come no one is fighting back? What's happening?

It begins to rain. It's getting dark. The column is not a column and the people behind me are desperate. I have a feeling that this hysteria could get us killed. We are still sliding down the river when we get the order to go back up the mountain. Up the mountain? Everybody turns and up we go. About five minutes of this and boom, mortars start falling and we can hear a battle, or at least guns going off quite nearby. Everybody panics, we turn, and back down the mountain/river we go. As we are flying down someone yells, 'Look! There's the enemy!' I look because I've never seen the enemy and I want to see what he looks like. I see men in uniforms on the other side of the river watching us. They don't look that different from the *compas* but I think I'll keep on sliding down the river.

It's quite dark by the time we get to the bottom. Everyone is all bunched up and Jacinto finally puts order to this mess and we get back into a column. We walk, all night, in the pouring rain on a path that has just been cut by the front of the column. What a night. Feet squooshing through the mud, bodies soaking wet and it's pitch black. Everyone holds on to the knapsack in front and we move slowly on a path that should you slip you'll go tumbling down who knows how far. The column stops sporadically, I guess they are hacking their way through the brush, and I can feel the person holding on to my knapsack suddenly rest her whole weight on her arms as she falls asleep holding on to my back.

At 05:00 hrs we are on top of some mountain. We are told that we have to get off that mountain and into that valley before dawn. Down we go. We get to a road and there are *compas* stationed along the way urging us to go faster and faster. It's light now and we can see and we're walking on a level surface.

We walk through a small village. I feel like I'm in some kind of a movie. Over 200 guerrillas, all covered in mud, come stumbling through town, running for their lives, supposedly, and the people in town wave to us and say good morning. They smile, we smile, we say good morning. Take care we say, you take care too and wave again and on we go. Very bizarre.

We are now in another town exposing our shrivelled-up feet to the sun. Jacinto came by and said to me, 'You are ordered to rest! We move out at 11:00 hrs and wait till you see the surprise we are going to have later this afternoon!' Food, we know it's going to be food. We haven't eaten in two days.

We arrive in Comalapa at 15:00 hrs. The town is completely controlled by the *compas*. The town people are friendly and don't seem to mind.

I'm sitting on the sidewalk in front of some houses where we are going to spend the night. I see all kinds of people I know and haven't seen in months. It's like a reunion. A *compa* with a bandaged hand stops to talk and tells us that yesterday during the river panic, it was them fighting. He's with the X-21 and a small group of them were just over the other side of that mountain when they bumped into another armed group. They called out, 'What battalion are you with?'

'You tell us first', yelled back the other group, 'who are you with?'

'No, you tell us first.'

Both groups continue walking towards one another and the other group is finally forced to identify themselves, 'We're with the guerrilla battalion.'

There is no battalion with that name and the *compas* realize it is the enemy. At this point they are quite close to one another. They start shooting and the *compa* telling us the story got a bullet through his hand. He said that they were on their way to some place and had not expected to bump into the enemy. Had we decided to leave an hour earlier we would have walked right into their arms – no pun intended. Had the group from the X-21 not appeared the enemy might have discovered us and pursued us as we went tumbling down the river. But by that time they were otherwise engaged. This is definitely a strange war.

Throughout the rest of the afternoon large groups of combatants come and go carrying M-60s, grenade launchers – a great demonstration of force. This is their territory, they control it, move in it by day. Very interesting. They control the town, the phones, transportation, everything. We eat a tasty rice dish and tortillas and then lay our plastics out and sleep. Hundreds of bodies sleeping on the sidewalks. It's very funny. What must these people think?

The RAN (night reconnaissance plane) circles over, very low, all night. Obviously they know we are here. At dawn three buses come from La Laguna. The *compas* stop them, hold them for a while and then tell them that they have to go back. Sorry, fellas, can't go through today. We have a war going on right now.

We are now in La Laguna, also controlled by the *compas*. There are tons of people and weapons everywhere.

We don't know yet what the enemy intends to do. They have forces in Zapotal, the Montañona, Las Vueltas, Amatillo, Tamarindo, Patanera and a couple other places.

It seems we will stay here until the enemy decides to move. From here we can go anywhere, even to Guatemala. There are scouts and several battalions in different places – all is under control.

Luis, the Spaniard, another *compa* and myself are sitting on a sidewalk when a drunk man from town comes up to us and gives us each an egg, saying, 'You people don't have anything, not even eggs.' Eggs in Spanish also means balls or guts. I thanked him for the egg and then said, 'These people may not have this type of eggs, but eggs they've got.' Who knows what he thought, he was very drunk and went mumbling back into his house.

We lay out our plastics on another sidewalk, then the RAN returns. At midnight we receive orders to move out. We walk three hours and arrive at a town called Los Prados. The population is asleep and we crash on their doorsteps.

In the morning the first order is to make breakfast with the food we all had to carry last night. I find the food situation extremely humorous. How can they be worried about the enemy when their main concern is assuring breakfast the following day?

It seems that the Atlacatl is moving to La Laguna. A battalion has appeared on the other side of the town and we don't know if they are elite or not. If not, they are there just to ensure the leaving of the Atlacatl. If elite, this could mean they are preparing to invade La Dos. Either way there is going to be fighting around here. As I write I can already hear it.

For the people living in these larger towns, not directly under FMLN control but living in their zone, what must they think of all this? The *compas* moving around in daylight, carrying enormous amounts of weapons, going off to fight, coming back and hanging around, talking and laughing and eating on their doorsteps. I should think it is totally different when the government troops come through the same towns. I would love to be in one when that happens but, of course, I never will.

I really think this *guinda* is great! In a way it's not a *guinda*, it's part of the way this war is fought. The battalion I've been moving with is the battalion of logistics and supplies. They even have several mules that we started out with, carrying a variety of ammo. The combatants come in and out taking what they need.

I think the main strategy these days has been to tease the enemy. The *compas* circle around them, go through them, move to another place, sit and wait. If the enemy moves, then they move, but never too far, and always with a little ambush here and one over there.

We are waiting for them to move again. If they move in this direction we will go further into La Dos, circle around and go back to our base. My feet are worthless, I have slept one night in four, but I'm having a great time. I love going through all these new towns, seeing more of Chalate. Needless to say many great shots, but who has film? God knows if my stuff was found or wiped out by the sun and rain. Nothing I can do about it. Just saw another shot: three men from this town are on the path with a rope, lassoing each other and giggling hysterically while the *compas* go up and down heavily armed. Quite a contrast.

Betio told me that María et al. ran off to the same place! Jesus, I would never do it again with that group.

Well, the *compas* played music and danced yesterday afternoon. Then we listened while other *compas* fought the Atlacatl. Then because Jacinto didn't know exactly what the enemy had in mind, he moved us into La Dos last night. What a bitch of a walk and we were not allowed to use our flashlights.

I have discovered my greatest fear in this war: walking on mountain paths in the dark. When we did it the other night, in the rain, the only thing that kept me going was that the column was inching along and we held on to the person in front. The things I saw in the dark during that walk were terrible. When word came 'careful, big hole on the left', I saw an enormous chasm. Many times I saw bleeding babies stretching out their arms to me, deformed faces near my head, bodies and animals of all kinds, moving in the night – terrifying images.

Last night the column was moving fairly fast and so I was on my own, and after several hours I freaked. Panic exuded from every pore of my body – I couldn't control it – and I lost all sense of direction and balance, and my imagination eventually made it impossible for me to continue. I knew I was exhausted but that didn't change anything.

I finally stepped out of the column and said to the night, 'I will not walk until the sun comes out. I won't, I won't, I won't. *Vale verga!*'

The column was ordered to continue. A few minutes later Sonia appeared.

'Give me your hand.'

'No! No, I will not move until the sun comes out!'

I knew I was being utterly ridiculous but at that point I didn't care. I felt that I had to let out some of the craziness that was wallowing inside of me. Everybody else acts like an idiot when the bombs or mortars fall – why can't I act like an idiot? I'm not endangering anybody's life. I have the right to be an idiot. I have the right to be crazy too!

'Come on, give me your hand.'

I did. She walked ahead, leading me, my body trembling. Twenty minutes later I calmed down. Everything was under control. Jesus, I don't know what got into me. . . But it's over, the invasion is over.

October

We got back today. Our bodies totally wiped out. We came by via the Montañona. It's true that it's beautiful way up there with the scarred pine trees, but what a climb! About an hour from our base we were informed that Juan had been killed. It was a real blow. We kept on walking. When I knew where I was I lay on the ground and let everybody pass. Then I slowly made my way down to Cordoncillo.

Suddenly it all seemed too much and I began to cry. My nerves had snapped and this great feeling of despair because of Juan's death broke inside of me. I stumbled down the mountain sweating and crying. Luis appeared – I don't know from where, I thought I was completely alone – and took my knapsack. I blurted out all the pent-up feelings and madness within. Luis stayed with me until I calmed down.

Juan was a Spaniard who had been fighting here for years and was accepted as a Salvadoran. He lost one of his legs in a battle early on, and so whenever there was a *guinda* he would go to a safe place by horse or he hid underground. This time he went by horse to an area near Zapotal. He was with 25 people of the masses who had little babies and kids, plus his own small armed group. When the Atlacatl took Zapotal they sent out scouts. Juan's group was too sure of itself and, not expecting the enemy to be anywhere nearby, made a fire to cook. The scouts discovered them and sent in some troops. Juan and four others were killed, 12 captured and the rest fled. It's too sad.

So now it's *guinda* storytelling time again and for me it's post-*guinda* blues again. Ah, shit. But we go on; they talk and I listen to the blues. . .

The masses are very demoralized with this last invasion. A number of them have gone to Honduras. I don't know what the organization can do to give them more confidence if there is going to be an invasion every month. I wonder how these invasions have differed from 1982 or 1983? Why do so many of them seem to be leaving? Is this what usually happens after invasions? When things get tough you go off for a while and then come back? How is Popular Power doing in all this mess? Is it falling apart? Who will tell me?

Duarte is changing tactics, telling his troops not to kill the people but to capture them. He sends out printed propaganda saying, 'We are going to save you from the guerrillas!' Obviously, capturing is better than killing as you can get more information that way. In the last two invasions 90 people have been captured and there have been a number of deserters. I am told that most deserters don't go to the enemy side, they just get tired of the hassles and go off to Honduras.

I have not bathed in ten days and still can't as I don't have a dry pair of bluejeans. My clothes are getting very tattered, my one boot was cut on a rock during that long night march. But my equipment is all right, so to speak. I unrolled the mud covered plastic and there was my bag with all my stuff tucked inside, damp but not soaking wet. Great! Just a little more fungus.

Summer is coming, blue skies are reappearing at dawn. The drying process will soon begin.

My emotions are getting frayed. Luis's concern for me as I wailed down the path yesterday was unexpected and deeply appreciated. It was also the first time I felt that someone cared about me since I arrived. Is it the world I'm in or the war, or both?

My emotional needs and my idea of relationships don't seem to be shared here. Or the people I'm with express them differently. But it's not just the peasants I have been living with. The few non-peasants I have met are not very tender nor very giving of themselves. Self-protection? You cannot get too close or care too much because each loss, and there are many, would further incapacitate you in your ultimate goal which is to win this war?

But here at Sonia's I am still amazed with the lack of reaction to Juan's death. He was well known and well liked in this battalion. He was jovial and warm and yet it is, 'Oh, Juan died? OK. Let me tell you my *guinda* story.' Maybe caring or the way I express it is cultural. I don't know. I guess it has to be. I mean, what the hell is death to a peasant? And I don't mean that he/she doesn't feel anything, but what is death to them? So many, so hard the life, so numbing. The priorities of the people I live with are eating, bathing, washing clothes, surviving. It's cultural and it has to do with the culture of poverty and war. I feel wasted and empty by all the poverty, especially the poverty of relationships.

I am beginning to understand what Julio and I talked about once: having to learn fear. Like any other emotion we have to live it in order to feel it. It's taken me eight and a half months to really feel it and my awareness of living in a war is intensified by it.

If I had to walk back to the capital, the same way I came, I would do so with a certain amount of fear because I know what I'm walking through now and then I didn't. Now I have a much better understanding of what this reality is. Juan's death really shook me because he was yet another *compa* I knew, because it made me realize how vulnerable we are and that the enemy is something to fear.

While I was thinking about fear, Marga, Jorge and Luis came by. For the first time since being here I was glad to see those internationalists. I now understand why, when there is a chance to get together, they do. Something has to be shared. Even they were tense and frightened by the invasions. And this particular group is not easily frightened.

Marga described the *guinda* of one of the hospitals. It was a total mess. They were almost killed. Laura (Juan's *compa*) and Oni, a doctor, got the wounded out and eventually found an underground hiding place, except the area they chose was also the enemy's choice. They could hear them talking right above them. Oni had two grenades and a pistol. They decided that if they were discovered they would use one grenade for the enemy, the other one for the injured and the pistol to shoot themselves (i.e., Oni and Laura). They sat for two hours with their eyes wide open and their hearts thumping.

Jorge said that Karla is now sure that since her *compa* was killed she will also be killed. We all whispered that we didn't want to die.

'I'll be damned if I die here,' said I.

'I don't want to die here or anywhere,' said Marga.

Laura also arrived. She is a Spanish nurse who came to El Salvador with Juan. We talked about Juan and she said that had she not been in this country, had not lived here, and been told of Juan's death, it would have been much harder to deal with. Being here, she said, one gets accustomed to it, one has a better understanding of death.

Laura wanted to go find Juan's body and bury it. Luis, two *compas* and I went with her. Eventually we found Juan and three other bodies. Juan's other leg, his arms and his head had been chopped off.

On the way back, that lovely road leading to Zapotal was no longer lovely to me. It was sad, ugly and evil. Another battle ground, another cemetery.

Now it seems that Duarte wants to have a dialogue with the FMLN in La Palma. This could be interesting. The masses say that Duarte wants a dialogue because Reagan ordered him to have it as it will help Reagan's re-election. But then Duarte is not known in this country for having a mind of his own. People joke about the fact that even though D'Aubuisson[19] is an evil person, he is a Salvadoran and makes his own decisions; Duarte, they say, sold his soul, nationality and country to the *gringos*.

I went up to Jacinto this afternoon. He was in a meeting with Douglas, Ricardo and another *comandante* I didn't know. They told me to sit down. I asked Douglas if he had any new information on getting me out be it the passport or walking to Honduras or whatever they had in mind. He said there was a batch of documents coming but he didn't think 'mine' was in it and that they still considered the passport as the safest way to get me out. He said Esteban should be coming soon and should have more information. We talked about the dialogue. Douglas asked me if I wanted to go.

'Of course I would like to go!'

'OK. María is going with a group from the masses,' he said. 'Coordinate the timing with her. Tell her that I want you to stay with her in front of the column and I also want you to change your appearance before you go into La Palma. You're going to be leaving soon and I don't want anybody to remember your face.'

OK, OK! I get to go to La Palma! Anything, even if it means walking up 48 mountains, but anything to get out of where I am.

Well, here we are about 10 kilometers from La Palma. I started out with María and two days later as I was sprawled out on the ground with everyone else, resting my head on my knapsack, a small column walked by and stopped in front of me. I looked up and recognized a couple of people but not the rest. A voice said, 'Eh, Taina, you want to come with us or are you too tired?' It was Esteban. He was leading the column and had long hair and a beard and I didn't recognize him.

I jumped up and said, 'Oh no! I'm coming, I'm coming!'

I discovered that I was walking with the *comandantes* who will be meeting with Duarte. Cmte Esteban (FPL), Cmte Nadia (PRTC),[20] Cmte Cienfuegos (RN) and someone from the FAL. Then there were their respective bodyguards and assistants, several *compas* from the Special Forces in charge of security for the top honchos, the Tepehuani band, Sergio, Justo from the radio and myself.

Nadia had a bad foot and walked with a cane, so no one walked very fast but neither was it slow. It was all new territory for me and some of it was quite beautiful. We went down into pretty valleys with little dairy towns and drank milk and ate cheese and then up another mountain.

We spent the night in Los Naranjos, a pretty little mountain village. We made a huge bonfire in the inner courtyard of an abandoned house and toasted tortillas, drank coffee and someone played the guitar. It was lovely. The next day we arrived at Miramundo, a tiny town on top of a mountain. This will be our base during the dialogue.

Ungo and Zamora[21] are expected at any moment as they will spend the night up here with us. The Tepehuani made a welcome banner and Susana found a bunch of flowers. The FMLN press and the rest of the receiving team went down the mountain to receive them. Down there they couldn't find Ungo and Zamora, then they heard that they were already going up the muddy road and so everybody went racing up. Panting and covered in mud they placed the banner and flowers over some rocks. Susana suddenly noticed that Ungo's name was written with an *H*. She covered the *H* with some flowers and all went well.

From where we are we can see the tallest mountain in El Salvador, El Pital. At night it is very cold here. Julio, Toño, Sergio and I talked one of the store owners into letting us stay in a little room in his house that no one was using. It is tiny, with a double bed, but it's out of the wind. We drew sticks to see who would sleep on the floor. Toño lost.

At dawn everyone was very excited and preparing for their entrance into La Palma. Ungo had brought three diplomats with him and they were daintily trying to clean off the mud from their shoes. It seems they did not sleep well here. Ungo and Zamora slept in a little house. The diplomats chose to sleep in the jeep.

Several *comandantes* went to bathe in the river. The water was ice cold. Ungo decided he was going to bathe with the *comandantes* and brought his overnight case under his arm. It was amusing. He was quite pleased to be bathing with them. He dried himself and took out his deodorant and rubbed each armpit. The guerrillas don't use deodorant so the scene was even more amusing and touching.

A section of the X-21 got into formation and the *comandantes*, Ungo and Zamora stood in front of the troops. Zamora gave a speech to the troops saying that it was as a result of their actions, their combat abilities, that they were now going down to La Palma to talk with the government forces. Without them, the combatants, none of this would have been possible. He ended his speech saying that they spent the night in the mountains instead of a hotel because it was their way of participating with the FMLN forces.

The Red Cross appeared in two cars and took all of the honchos to La Palma.

Everybody else that was going, went. I stayed. When I knew I was going to La Palma and had to go disguised, I gathered up the hair of a *compa* that Sonia was cutting off. It was thick, black Indian-type hair and I pasted it onto a strip of scotch tape. Up here I put it on around my forehead and wrapped a cloth over my head. I was hoping to get some dark glasses but none could be found. I went over to Douglas in my wonderful disguise and he looked at me, smiled, and said, 'Nope, Taina, it won't do.' At least there is a television here and I can watch some of it.

It was quite a show. Around 50,000 people came from all over the country. María went with 115 from the masses. Then there were the FMLN/FDR and their security, in mufti, the Christian Democrats and the Salvadoran military, also in mufti. No weapons were allowed within a radius of ten kilometers but as the *compa* in charge of security for the honchos told me, there were hidden pistols all over town.

The Tepehuani went the night before and spent the whole night playing music and singing. Toño and Julio spent most of their time giving interviews to the national and international press. They also kept bumping into people they knew. Julio is Zamora's brother and knew many people. Toño was walking down the street and bumped into two of his aunts. He comes from an upper-class family. His aunts were thrilled to see him. They couldn't wait to get back to San Salvador and tell his mother that he was alive and well and looking very handsome. 'Oh, you look like a *comandante*!' they said ever so pleased. I was told that when the *comandantes* were walking into the church (where the meeting was held) and when they left, people would reach out and touch them, saying, 'Oh, I touched a *comandante*!'

The people of La Palma, I am told, are very pro-FMLN. When Ochoa, military head of Chalatenango, came to town two days before the dialogue to speak to the population, the people went into their houses and shut the door. He had to demand that they leave their houses and listen to his speech. When he was finished the soldiers waved to the people as they left. The people did not respond and returned to their houses and shut the door. Throughout the day of the dialogue the people from town gave food, cigarettes, sodas, whatever they could, to the guerrillas.

According to the FMLN the day in La Palma was a success. Not only were the people who came hoping for a real dialogue, as everyone is tired of the war, but it was a chance for many of them to 'see' the guerrillas and interact with them. They were the main attraction. Mixed with all of the excitement was a lot of tension – two armies met and had to act civilly to each other. But there was no incident.

I saw some of it on television. The meeting itself was held behind closed doors. But I saw the *comandantes* and Duarte and his people leave the church. Cienfuegos and Ungo came out first and the crowd roared, 'Ungo, Ungo, Ungo.' They both gave a speech and everybody clapped and yelled. When Duarte came up to give his speech most of the people had turned their backs and were getting ready to leave. It was funny. Next to the church, there was a little platform with Duarte's party-people so when he came to the microphone his little group yelled, 'Duarte, Duarte, Duarte.' But it was rather feeble. And then to see the people leaving, not at all interested in what he had to say. The FMLN had come, had met with the government, and were leaving. The show was over.

I think Duarte was taken aback by the reaction of the population today.

The amazing thing is that all of this was organized in ten days. The government forces invaded the zone and on 5 October, the last day of the invasion, Duarte said, OK, boys, we'll meet in La Palma on the 15th.

Everyone was quite up with the experience. It seems that there was much support, interest, respect and awe by the people for the FMLN/FDR. And so the long march back was full of stories and laughing all the way.

Going up one of the steepest mountains just before La Una, Toño, Julio and a couple of others were making jokes about all the different professions the *compas* were going to have after the triumph. Toño said, 'Douglas will open up a tourist agency in the capital. Specialty: mountain climbing and scenic places!' We roared with laughter as we suffered up the mountain.

I am very sick. I have a fever. My body, bones and muscles ache, my hands burn, I am dying of thirst and my mind is going crazy. Crazy. The fever comes and goes. The acid taste in my mouth makes it impossible to eat. I don't know what I have, but it's getting worse. I don't have the shakes so it can't be malaria. I haven't slept in two nights nor eaten in three days. I am on the verge of tears and can't hold back most of the time. I'm falling apart. I'm not going to eat anymore. I'm going on a hunger strike. I will not eat with Sonia's people again. This place is filthy, they vomit in the room, pee in the corners or outside the door, blow their noses in their hands, don't wash the dishes, no, no I can't take it anymore.

They are unaware, insensitive. There's no compassion here. None. Is it cultural, is it class? What is it? Why is there no compassion here? Why? Jesus Christ, I'll go crazy here, I will, because I can't take it anymore. It's not my world and it's not my war. I am imprisoned in the front and I'm going to go on a hunger strike because Taina has reached her limit. She has. Tenderness, compassion – Oh God I will go mad. Must always have a few friends wherever one is because otherwise living is too terrible.

My mind is going in circles. I can't control it. I've been spending hours talking to someone in my head, in Spanish, about what I'm going through, why it's destroying me, what it means to be 'awaiting' for five months. Over and over, and I can't stop. I think I'm breaking down. I've lost control. My head is burning again, and I can't stop explaining my pain, my anxiety, my sadness. I can't stop explaining how my soul is being destroyed by a hunger for gentleness, for compassion. I have to explain it to someone. But there is no someone so I explain it to my mind.

I don't know if I'm delirious or having a nervous breakdown. But something is happening over which I have no control. I am dying from too much aloneness, I am crying from too much sadness, I am despairing from the excess of poverty in all things – it is too much. Which is hottest: my tears or my face?

But let me explain it again, maybe you didn't understand. Let me tell you what it feels like, what it looks like, what the colors are inside my soul, why my heart is shrivelling up. Maybe I can put it another way, maybe if I, but no, it's very simple, it's the lack of humanity as I know it, it's the lack of caring as I understand it, it's an aloneness that has lost all walls – boundless. Let me explain the pain that shoots through my legs when I walk, the pain in my heart when I sit in darkness. Let me explain what someone from another world might need once in a while, let me explain why I'm falling apart, why my stoicism has crumbled, why I'm going mad, why this prison is killing me. Oh, let me explain it, please!

It's midnight and I've begun to shake violently. I don't believe that anybody can shake this way. It's all theater. But it isn't. Yet maybe it is. It's too humorous. I must stop acting. This is too much Taina. Stop shaking. I can't. Lighting a cigarette is very difficult, the flame jerks violently and I think if somebody sees me they'll laugh with me. This is too much shaking.

I must have malaria. Four pills, that's all I have. I'll take them. Maybe I can get eight more tomorrow. I'll take a sleeping pill too. Count sheep they say. But sheep are a little ridiculous here. I'll count rocks, Chalate rocks.

I counted 340 Chalate rocks and went into a deep sleep for four hours. I feel more like a real person this morning. I'm drinking coffee and have been given four more quinine pills. Not enough, but hopefully they will do the trick. Oh God! The last three days have been utter madness. Thank God for sleeping pills. Why didn't I take them on the first night? Too crazy to think straight.

Three days ago was exactly 15 days since I stopped taking anti-malaria pills. I've been on them for over a year and decided to stop. Among the many possible consequences of taking them are sterility and blindness. My eyes are very important to me. So I stopped. I guess I'll start taking them again.

Well, the one and famous Lt Colonel Domingo Monterosa[22] has just been blown up in a helicopter in Morazán. ERP did it. It seems that he has passionately tried to destroy the Venceremos radio for some time now and about an hour and a half ago he said by radio, 'I have destroyed the Venceremos radio.' An hour later the Venceremos radio said, 'We have destroyed Monterosa.' So be it.

Gustavo came through and we had a short chat. He is no longer head of the X-21 battalion but working in the upper echelons of military command. I'm not surprised. The kid is bright. He told me that now Duarte is going to have to take the FMLN more seriously and will consequently attack with more vehemence. Therefore the FMLN troops will have to increase their mobility. One moment here, one moment there. Back to basic but developed guerrilla tactics. He also said that they are going for a monthly enemy casualty rate of 500 soldiers.

If the troops are going to be more mobile than they already are, the masses are really going to have to organize themselves. I hear that more and more are going to Honduras.

María just came through and said that about 500 have left but there are over 2,000 still here; elections are being prepared and life goes on. Nothing changes.

The northern winds have come, summer is here, the air is fresh, the sky blue and flowers everywhere. At least in the next invasion there won't be any more rain, mud or full rivers. I hope.

Sandra, a Spanish internationalist, is here visiting. We went to the river to swim/bathe and talked for hours. I asked her if she also felt here a lack of tenderness, of affection, or if it was just me. She said she felt the same. She worked in some Salvadoran refugee camps in the past and didn't feel it there, but here, yes. She said that if she had come alone (she came with four other Spaniards) she would have turned right around and gone home. For a long time after they arrived nobody bothered with them, no questions, no interest in who they were or what they were going to do here. But they had each other.

I said that I thought, perhaps, this lack of affection/tenderness – aside from living in a war – was the consequence of being a peasant, of living a brutal life. No? How can you be tender in the midst of all this harshness and misery?

To be a peasant is just too bloody miserable. It is. I don't expect them to have my needs or my crazy mind but I do expect them to have the right and the dignity to live like human beings. A pet dog in a middle-class home has more than they have and that's not right. You don't need lots of money or cars or personal computers to be human in this world. But you need to be treated like one to be one.

Wrote to Esteban yesterday and received a note to meet him. He told me that he is meeting with someone today who is going to the capital to discuss my papers. I told him that I didn't want to stay any longer where I was and that I refused to *guindiar* with the same group twice. Why? Because something inside me says never do it with the same group. Plus, each new group I go to is moving in the direction I will have to go to get out once my documents arrive. No? He smiled and said, 'OK, to the radio you go.' Exactly what I had in mind.

He wrote a note to Elias, head of the radio, saying: 'Here is Taina, she will stay with you while she waits.' So be it. One month, two months? Esteban said he didn't know but that it had to be on its way.

OK, I will not lose faith. How can I? Then I heard the story of how the whole *Chile* was almost wiped out in the last invasion. Good God! We're talking about all the top honchos of the FPL! There they were when Douglas suddenly realized that they were surrounded by the enemy. The enemy, of course, didn't know that they were surrounding anybody. Supposedly Douglas looked at everyone and said, 'What the fuck do we do now?' They got out. I wonder how? This war is incomprehensible but then I guess all wars are.

I went over to see Luis and tell him that I was moving to the radio. He is as desperate as I am. He said that if his documents don't come by November he's going to walk to Costa Rica. Why don't we swim? I said.

November

Here I am at the radio. Another new group of people. Elias, I have decided, is a very nice person. When I arrived he said, 'This is your house.' I said that although I was wiped out psychologically I could help out – do something. He said, 'Just rest, take it easy.' Right, which means I shall continue to do what I've been doing – awaiting.

It's very pretty here. We're high up and there are pine trees growing in red earth. Our quarters are lean-tos or thatched huts. We are not plane visible. The kitchen is down by the river with a green tarp over it. It's nice and so are the people. I'm drinking coffee and it's communal coffee – neat! Everybody who wants some can have some. This is the way I like things to be. Everyone in the kitchen is talking about past invasions and where the enemy could enter this time. I don't much like this kind of talk, but this is the reality. If not this topic, what other one? Actually, it's just like being with the battalions, the topic of conversation is the last battle, the last *guinda* – nothing has changed except that I have lived through a lot more. Nothing has changed, only my head.

I know that the invasions in 1982 were much more terrible than anything I've lived through, but these are all I know. The possibility of dying becomes more real and fear becomes part of the day-to-day. After the fifth invasion does the fear change? I don't know, perhaps it only becomes more familiar.

Aside from the radio people and their cooks and security, the Tepehuani band is here, a Swiss woman called Lisa, who has just entered the front, and myself.

Yesterday afternoon we were heavily attacked by mortars. We are now in a state of alert. One of the Cazador battalions is in Concepción de Quesaltepeque but no one anywhere else. Then today two A-37s bombed us. We all carried the things we wouldn't take on a *guinda* – my equipment, musical instruments, and the radio equipment – to a well-built underground vault. We prepared for *guinda* number three. In the evening we met in the kitchen, and Justo, second in command of the radio, told us what was happening militarily and how the column would be organized should we get the order to move out. Then he passed out plastic bags filled with powdered milk mixed with sugar – called operative rations – to each of us.

This morning the situation is better – whatever that means – and if it continues we will unearth things tomorrow. Justo says that the enemy is acting very defensively. They have been hit very hard these last two weeks including the death of Monterosa, five helicopters out of commission and many casualties. In the last four days 47 bombs have fallen in Cabañas, Cuscatlán and Chalate. All indiscriminate.

Last night we were given the order to move out. We destroyed the camp and walked down the mountain with two horses carrying radio equipment so that they can transmit while on *guinda*. The moon was out and it was a nice walk – only a couple of hours – and then we spent the night somewhere.

We are not on a *guinda*, we are on a *pre-guinda*; the radio is treated with extra caution. The Belloso battalion and the 4th Brigade are in Dulce Nombre, Tehutla and La Laguna. They are trying to take El Común but haven't yet. There are battles. The soldiers in La Laguna wanted to take the Montañona, but the X-21 didn't let them and they retreated back to town. It could be that the action will be only in La Dos, although this is doubtful. It could be another invasion and the enemy is going to cut off La Dos and then come in through Las Flores, etc.

At 14:00 hrs we stood in a column ready to start another walk. We were told that we would be walking for six hours. After walking 45 minutes we were told that that was it. The enemy didn't advance, so why walk more than necessary? We were near the post office and messenger camp so we invaded their kitchen and made coffee with milk – great! At 17:45 hrs, only 45 minutes late for the afternoon broadcast, they did their radio show. It was interesting. The horses had been carrying a small motor, gasoline and equipment. They started the motor and there were Arnulfo with his mixer and Guillermo with his voice and papers standing on either side of a low stone wall.

Being with the radio is all right. You get lots of info on enemy activity as the radio is a priority and well protected. Consequently, they go on *preventivos* as well as *guindas*. For the radio people it's the only time they get to walk around and see the countryside.

We returned from whence we came. Enemy is still in La Laguna but it's not the elite, only the 4th. The *compas* are still in the Montañona so if the enemy moves up we will still have time to get out.

Upon arriving at the old camp Lisa, Mati, two other *compas* and myself found a canvas hidden in the bushes and tied it to what was still standing of one of the huts. It started pouring and the five of us, wrapped up in our covers on the ground, were thinking we were ever so lucky, ever so dry. Well, the canvas was not taut and filled up with water and suddenly it collapsed on us with gallons of water. Very nice. We got soaking wet. My turn for the nightwatch came, I did it, then took a sleeping pill, wrapped my wet self in the plastic and went to sleep.

Here at the radio everybody does nightwatch. A new list is made up each evening. Duty lasts from 30 minutes to an hour depending on how many people are here. We do it in pairs, usually the same pairs. The time gets later and later till you're first on duty again at 18:00 hrs. My partner is the flute player of the band, we have an M-16, which neither of us really knows how to use but what the hell. We know there is more security further from the camp.

I have been thinking that with all of this waiting and the ensuing frustration I lose a certain perspective on this war. I lose a certain aspect of the heroism that exists, that has to exist for this type of war to be fought. I mean, here are a very poor and simple people fighting a US-backed and financed army. I lose this vision at times, especially these last three months. The war becomes quotidian, becomes routine. The struggle, the sacrifice, the battles, the *guindas*, the deaths, the bombings, all become everyday occurrences. But it is this dailiness of the war that only reinforces the fact that all revolutionary wars can only be fought by people who are seeking changes in their own society. Revolutionaries are basically common, ordinary, everyday folk, reflecting a cross section of their country. The intellectual left and the right have idealized them, one as great, the other as evil.

I don't know, maybe one of these days when I am outside I will be able to put it all together.

I have just written a rather severe note to Esteban saying that Justo wants to keep my film and equipment underground, for security reasons, instead of putting them in and taking them out all of the time. So, if I'm not going to be leaving this month, having my film sweat underground after all the rain it has had to endure these last six months means that there is nothing worth saving, so why am I waiting for documents, why don't I just present myself at the US embassy in the capital? I am beginning my tenth month, goddamn it!

Hell, who knows? I don't.

Lisa just gave me a pair of underpants! Since someone stole my pair I've only had one and it makes bathing communally very difficult. One day I have underpants the other I don't. Now everything is very fine indeed.

Lisa and I are sharing a hut that we put back together. It has a plastic on the roof and sides so we don't freeze at night. This is the first night that I haven't frozen up here. She brought a sleeping bag which is great for this climate. But if she goes elsewhere it will be terrible: hot and filled with fleas. Here it's too cold for them. I like Lisa. We spend a lot of time together. I also like Jorge, the musician, and during our nightwatch we talk: time passes quickly and another day arrives.

I aired all my equipment and film, again. I don't know if I'm being ridiculous or not – probably – one cannot live by hope alone, but one does anyway.

Every afternoon the Tepehuani rehearse under the pine trees. It's very nice listening to flutes, guitars and the songs. We all know the songs by heart and we sing along with them.

Then it's to the kitchen where we all congregate, each bringing our plastic bag of goodies. Mine these days are lemons, garlic and margarine. Margarine is the latest thing, we buy it in little sticks, two by one inches, and I put some on a toasted tortilla, with cut-up garlic, salt and lemon juice – it's the best! But what I like is that everybody has their plastic bag and we sit around pulling our goodies out and talking.

I just got a note from Esteban: the passport is on its way! Should not take longer than 15 days. I don't know whether to be happy or scared shitless. It better be good, it better be European, it better . . . Oh hell, I don't know what to feel. I just want to get out of here.

It's the great battle of Suchitoto day! As of 12:00 hrs three helicopters have been shot down, four hit and one A-37 damaged. The enemy is bombing the hell out of the town: church, school, hospital, municipal market. The radio has been going all morning. (Usually they broadcast at 07:00, 12:00 and 17:00 hrs. But when there is a special battle they broadcast as long as it happens or as long as they keep getting new information.) COPREFA, the Salvadoran military press office, and the deathsquads have threatened all national radios if they talk about it. Sonora radio seems to be the only one to keep coming out with information, even using the Farabundo as source.

It's interesting to see the radio functioning under these conditions. We listen to their reporters coming in with new info, and then we hear a bit of what the enemy is saying. It's quite dramatic. I'd love to be there. No press is being allowed in for the moment.

The battle of Suchitoto is over, and for the FMLN it was another success. They had two objectives: (1) to eliminate 17 military posts within the town, and (2) to hit the helicopters as hard as possible. Total enemy casualties were 102. The government forces are trying to blame the FMLN for the destruction of the church, school, hospital, etc. It's going to be hard to fabricate evidence for that. I even heard a tape of the enemy telling their planes to bomb the press cars. They didn't, but they tried to scare them. I bet the government forces are not feeling too well – they've had heavy losses over the last three weeks and then they get hit with Suchitoto.

It's *guinda* number three! At 04:00 hrs right after Lisa and I finished nightwatch, the mortars began to fall. There is something eerie about mortars falling in the early dawn. We packed our *guinda* knapsacks, destroyed the lean-to, and took what had to be stored to the vault. By 07:00 hrs we were all ready, went down part of the mountain to a little camp, and had breakfast with mortars and rockets falling all over the place. Then on to the same places we had gone to on our preventive *guinda*.

At 19:00 hrs we began a long walk. The moon was out and we could use our flashlights but we were walking through stony terrain covered thickly with *zacate*, a tall grass that cuts, prickles and stings your skin. At 03:00 hrs we stopped for a rest, then walked four more hours to a place called Portillo del Norte, a little hamlet up in the mountains. Here we are camped out on a rocky field, covered with lots of trees, just outside of town.

We can hear combat here and there, but nothing very close. The radio is doing its noon broadcast under a tree. We don't know what we'll do next. It seems unlikely that the Belloso would come over here without reinforcements in Los Ranchos, El Cerrón, etc. No one knows what the Belloso is doing, as they've already been on the road for eight days and are very tired. One idea is that they thought they would do a quickie through here, thinking that the *compas* would still be around Suchitoto, but, as usual, they were wrong.

During lunch Justo was saying that in the beginning of the war the enemy used French bomber planes, and the *compas* looked at them and thought, how do we fight that? They got used to them. Then came the A-37s and the *compas* thought, *puta mierda*, now what do we do? Then came the helicopters and the airborne transporters and the *compas* thought, *vale verga*, and figured out how to deal with them (27 airborne soldier casualties in Suchitoto) and how to bring the choppers down, and are no longer afraid of them. The learning process involved is fascinating. In four years these kids have learned a hell of a lot – from wooden guns to shooting down helicopters. Not bad.

We have been waiting all morning for word on whether we move or not. The Belloso remain in the same places, they have taken certain mountain tops in this direction but are not moving. From where we are we can see the helicopters bringing in food and supplies.

If they don't move, we don't move. They have three options for their exit: (1) through Las Vueltas – we don't move; (2) through Las Flores – we move a little; and (3) through Los Ranchos – we walk eight hours. *Guindiando* with the radio is so preventive that it's no fun – actually, it's boring as hell. I much preferred running around with Jacinto.

We are in the fifth day of sitting under the trees doing nothing. The helicopters come and go, and during one crazy moment I thought of running down the mountain with a huge sign saying: journalist needs a lift out of here.

Well, we're back, just below the old camp, and here we'll stay for a while. Another pretty place with the wind whistling through the pine trees, another pretty day.

I was just down in the kitchen making my usual can of coffee when Justo appeared and said, 'Elias has something for you.'

'What? A letter from Esteban?'

'No, something else. I think you'd better go up and see Elias.'

Oh God! Pant. The passport! Pant, pant. Could it be? I won't think about it. It's probably a letter, just a letter. My heart thumped as I walked into Elias's room. He smiled and handed me a manila envelope.

Inside was a passport with my picture – shit – and a note from Esteban: 'Not what I was hoping for but as far as passports are concerned this one will get you safely out of here and around this part of the world. Elias will help you with your 'story'. I hope to see you before you leave.'

Trembling, I looked at Elias and said, 'I can't pass for this nationality.'

Elias said his first reaction had been the same. Then he talked to Roberto, a *compa* recently arrived into the front, and Roberto said, no problem, she can pass easily. Roberto knows the country and will spend as many days as are needed to tell me everything about 'my' country. (This is necessary in case the powers that be should question or be suspicious of me or my passport – if so I need to be very convincing.)

I always thought, in a romantic sort of way, that it would be rather neat to be a spy and use false papers – you know, very 007 and exciting – but now that it seems that I will really have this opportunity I am freaked out. God, the adventure is never ending. Even getting out couldn't be something less dramatic. That would be too boring, eh?

Her age is close enough to mine, that's no problem. Her signature is very artistic and I think I can reproduce it. But she's a professional. How the hell am I going to pass for a professional speaking guerrilla Spanish these days and wearing tattered clothes? Huh? It's a brand new passport, never been used. But is it well done? How should I know? I've heard so many stories of documents made by the *compas* that weren't quite good enough. It's either a good or a bad one – extremes, always extremes. Which one is mine? I'll find out. My entrance stamp into El Salvador is for December 12, so I can't leave until the 18th, and I can't leave with any of my equipment or film. Damn!

Well, things don't seem as bad as I thought, in one area. Roberto tells me that my looks and my Spanish are perfectly suitable. The important thing is the role and the belief in it. The important thing is to believe that I am that person, no matter what happens. I am, I am, I am she. I am to learn everything, but everything, about the country.

What really makes me sad is not being able to take my equipment, film and notebooks. I hope Esteban has some good ideas about how to get them out.

I am completely in tatters: my socks have huge holes, my jeans – I only have one pair now – are worn through in the seat. I'm not even dressed well enough for this front.

Things are looking very interesting. Duarte seems to be up against a wall. The FMLN has proposed a national ceasefire. The contradictions within the regime are becoming more acute. The working class is getting more and more organized around the question of negotiations and demanding peace. Who knows what this revolution is going to come up with. *Sui generis* to a large extent. History changes from within and moves, at times, in incomprehensible ways, but the movement is from within, the rhythm is unique according to a people. There are no ballroom rules.

But I still think that a lot more political work needs to be done with these people. Whom they are fighting they know very well. What they are fighting for becomes diffuse or out there somewhere. I think the whole educational level in this war needs to be raised, needs to be taken seriously, because a new stage is being entered and they are going to need it.

I am to be transferred to La Dos. I'm getting there! Roberto will go up the following week to finish my lessons. My equipment, notebooks and film are in Elias's hands. I wonder if I will ever see them again?

December

Here I am at logistics and supplies of La Dos – back to a peasant environment. It was a nice break being at the radio, Lisa and I got along very well and time passed rapidly.

I know these last days are not going to be easy. I worry that there will be another invasion and it will be too late to leave on this passport. At least the number of days I can stay in the country has not been circled in yet but I don't think this nationality would be given more than two weeks. After I worry about getting out of the front I can worry about getting out of the country and then in and out of Guatemala and so on. Great.

Duarte finally agreed to another dialogue. But this time he decided there would be no party, meaning people. The meeting was held, again in a church, outside of San Salvador. Access to the road leading to the church was blocked by the military and only a small group of the 'Mothers of the Disappeared' and the press were allowed through. Each group was given its own cordoned-off section far from the church. Duarte seems to be afraid of the Salvadoran people.

Esteban gave a great speech after the meeting – I heard it on a national station – and it was enthusiastically received.

A horse died down there somewhere and I'm watching the buzzards. It's really true that they whoosh just like mortars when they dive down through the air. That whooshing sound that is so comforting with mortars because as long as they're whooshing they're not going to fall on your head. It's when you hear the whoosh up ahead and then silence that you have to worry. But it's amazing how these birds sound like mortars. Life is definitely full of wonders.

Jesus, did it mortar last night! Over 100 of them fell all around us. All within 45 minutes. While Paraíso was mortaring us the barracks in Chalatenango city were mortaring La Una. The 100 was not counting the ones that fell there, which we could also hear.

What a whooshing evening. Today we are in a state of emergency. Enemy is in Dulce Nombre where they've been for several days. Everybody is talking *guinda*. After seeing all the disorganization in this camp I decided that I'm not going on a *guinda* with these folks. So I sent a note to Turcios telling him that. This afternoon someone came to take me to Turcios's camp.

Today things are calmer and I feel a lot safer here at La Dos military head-quarters. The enemy has not moved nor increased its forces and no mortars last night. But who knows? If we go on a *guinda* I can't go running with all my stuff; if I leave it here and we are near a highway and they want to send me off then I won't have my stuff. Wait and see what the enemy does. Wait and see. I still have two weeks but it could be two months, it could be forever.

Turcios' people have been together, I would assume, for some time, but when it comes to doing nightwatch they act like they've never done it before. The incredible thing is that about half of them don't know how to read the time, so the whole night is one chaotic mess! The amount of time each has to do depends on how many we are, and every night the number changes. Let's say we have to do 38 minutes. (I am not being facetious, the *compa* who prepares the list each night takes his math very seriously.) A *compa* is woken up, given a watch, he goes out and guesses what 38 minutes are. Sometimes it's an hour and sometimes it's ten minutes. Crazy! What the hell, war à la peasant.

But it really is quite a mess here and it is in other places, and considering all the chaos, it's a wonder that they manage so well. Which makes me wonder about the government soldiers. They must have their own chaos too. I can see how the *gringos* couldn't fathom the mind and way of the Vietnamese, but the Latin style must drive them up the wall. I wonder what they think of the troops, both sides talking and yelling and singing out to each other? How does one understand this madness? How do they advise it?

During the first six months of Duarte's regime the government forces have suffered 3,390 casualties, and 174 prisoners were taken by the FMLN; 500 M-16s or equivalent, 80 M-60s, two 120s and 48 PRT77 radios were captured. Four helicopters were shot down, two 'push&pulls', eight helicopters and one A-37 were hit. There were 119 combats, 57 confrontations and 156 ambushes by the FMLN (sources: Farabundo and Venceremos radios).

The enemy is close by again. Turcios got back last night and we talked. He said that if everything is fixed he'll prepare my exit now. But nothing's fixed yet! I'm beginning to question whether Esteban is going to come through or not. And if he doesn't, what do I do?

Roberto arrived this morning with all of my work and camera bag. What does this mean? Oh, well, continue with my lessons.

It's one big family sitting in the sun getting rid of the cold bones from the night before. People playing cards, laughing, sleeping, radios playing rock and roll, the days pass, the airplanes pass, the war passes at its own family pace.

Luis arrived. He finally received a passport too! We sit in the sun working on our signatures. Both Luis and I have the same fear: that it will be the Costa Ricans that will see through the passports. But, if that happens, they, at least, won't torture or kill us. Once in jail I'll call friends. Everything is going to work out all right, she said for the tenth time.

The days continue to go by, the enemy remains where it is. God knows how we get out of here. It is now the 19th. Yesterday Chacho, who is leaving because he is very ill, Luis and I thought that we would have to leave, walking, through Guazapa. Then we got word via the radio that we were not to move and that messages were on their way. So here we are waiting to see what the organization is thinking about. Chacho is adamant that we leave as clean as possible. Don't take notebooks or film. To me that means the end of it all – one year of my life lost.

Word has just come to start the process for our leaving. A *compa* is going off to buy Luis and me some clothes.

My clothes arrived this morning. I am, supposedly, an upper middle-class professional on vacation and this is what I wear on my short tour of scenic Chalatenango: a pair of black linen-like jeans (at least they are cotton), a baby-blue/polyester/puffy little sleeves/disgusting frilly blouse, a pair of little black-cloth Chinese, plastic-soled shoes with bright red flowers embroidered on top, a little cardboard bag with a roll of toilet paper, a camera and a pair of shorts in it. Yeah. . .

'It's the best I could do,' the *compa* smiled shyly.

OK, OK, I can handle it, but not the blouse. No way will I wear that fluffy polyester thing. No way. One of the radio *compas* had a red shirt that was a bit more my style, at least it was made of cotton. I asked her if she would like to exchange the red for the blue. No problem. She loved the blue one. I tried on my new outfit, and everybody thought I looked fantastic. I was trembling inside thinking that I would never make it through with these clothes.

Luis got a pair of normal jeans and a decent T-shirt, but no shoes. There weren't any his size. He's got big feet.

Susana arrived with her entourage and met first with Luis, then with me.

'Upon arriving at the capital', Susana said, 'I want you to go directly to Metro Centro (a huge shopping center) and buy decent clothing. Then you will leave the country by bus – don't go near Ilopango airport – via such-and-such a place. You are not to go the same route as Luis.'

'Why?'

'Because Luis has a European passport.'

What the hell is that supposed to mean?

'Luis will take all of your equipment in the camera bag but no film and no notebooks.'

'Why can't he take my film and notebooks?'

'Security, Taina, security. Give me all of your stuff and an address to contact you in the US and we will arrange to have it sent to you.'

A *compa* produced a big plastic bag.

'But, Susana, this is my life! I can't leave without it!'

'Taina, your life is you and that is what we are concerned with and that is what you are going to take with you. Now give it to me and get going.'

I gave it to her.

Luis and I were taken to Jessica's base: a hill of dried bean leaves under a big tree looking out on a dry riverbed, on the side of a mountain, outside of some town. It's a pretty place and softer than anything I've sat on in months. Jessica is in charge of getting people in and out of the front.

She read Susana's note and told us to rest. She was going to town and see about a pair of shoes for Luis and prepare our exit. Food would be sent up to us and she would see us in the evening.

She returned in the evening and said she had ordered the shoes. As to our exit, she was worried, because there was enemy movement in several places including in the town where we are to catch the bus to get out. Great.

The following evening, Christmas Eve, the shoes arrived. They were the biggest pair they could find: huge, black, pointed horrible things. I started laughing hysterically because I had never seen a pair of shoes like this except, perhaps, in an old 1950s movie. Luis was hysterical for other reasons and said that he would not wear them, that he would go barefoot before putting them on his feet.

There we were sitting on the bean leaves after being in a war for one and a half years (Luis) and one year (me), we were both using fake passports for the first time in our lives, we were about to get out after a very long wait, the enemy was all around, the final process seemed out of control and we were hysterical with fear, tension and apprehension.

Jessica looked at us, at the shoes, smiled and said, 'OK. You're going to have to wait some more. I'll order a pair from the capital.' Then she told us that tonight we were going to go down to one of the houses and have a little Christmas dinner.

A nun had come from the capital to spend Christmas with a family, and we had a quiet meal that neither Luis nor I was up to celebrating. Throughout the night mortars fell and firecrackers went off. The two are not that different in sound. Lying on the bean heap, looking up at the stars, I wondered why

Salvadorans, in the midst of a war, choose to set off those big bang-bangs. Luis was freaking out and I told him to calm down and listen to the difference between them.

Christmas Day Luis and I hung around the bean mound. A *compa* brought us a little bottle of homemade firewater made from corn. Why not? I hadn't had any alcohol the whole time I'd been in the front; I didn't think it would be too much against the rules if I had a little before I left. We sipped the stuff while we worked on our signatures. We started making jokes about arriving at the hotel we were told to stay in and asking where the river was and if they had a gourd, about wondering off into the garden looking for the perfect spot to pee, etc.

That night we decided we wanted to leave the next morning, pretending that we had spent Christmas in La Palma. Jessica arrived and said that the shoes had not yet arrived, the enemy was in La Palma and in the town we were to leave from, and she did not know what she should do. During the afternoon we had filled in our days allowed in the passports because we were sure we were going to leave soon and now?

The following morning the shoes did not arrive but Jessica said they were on their way, on one of the buses. In the evening they arrived. They fit. We said, 'OK, we go tomorrow, somehow, but we go tomorrow.' Later on Jessica returned and said that we would leave at 03:00 hrs. But, we had to work on our 'story' so as to explain what we were doing in this part of the world should anybody ask. She also informed us that the *compa* who had brought the shoes would go back on the bus with us to make sure that we arrived in the capital safely.

Getting Out

We don't sleep. At 02:00 hrs we take a bath and put on our new clothes. I leave my boots and whatever is still wearable with Jessica and off we go down the mountain. Luis is carrying my camera bag with my equipment and I am walking in my little Chinese slippers. We pass quietly through a town, meet the *compa* who is to go with us, arrive at a crossroads and wait for the 05:00 hrs bus.

There we are, Luis and I, standing in the dark, lost in our own deep thoughts, when suddenly the heavens light up with fireworks and a band begins to play. I don't believe it! I start laughing quietly thinking this is too insane, we are caught inside a Gabriel García Márquez novel! I don't believe this is happening. Here we are at dawn in the middle of nowhere with our funky clothes and our funky passports, and a band is playing and fireworks are going off. Luis is not at all amused.

The bus arrives and minutes later we drive through a little town and there, in a little public square, in a little band shell, no less, is a little band playing.

It is usually at bridges that the military has its check points. We go over several and I see soldiers lounging around in the sun. Too early, I guess, for stopping traffic and anyway it's the end of the year.

About two hours later, a half hour from San Salvador, the bus is stopped. Everybody out. The *compa* mutters for us to go first and stay calm. We get off the bus and stand in a line by the side of the road. A soldier checks all IDs but ignores Luis and me. I feel like a complete idiot with my little Chinese shoes. There are many soldiers and one big honcho strutting and flexing his muscles and eyeing me. Shit, here goes. He struts some more, looking at the line of people, then at me, then at the top of the bus, then back at me, and then in a booming voice says, 'I would love to know just how many pounds of explosives are being carried on top of this bus. Yeah. . .' Strut, strut. 'I bet many pounds, you fucking guerrillas.' Strut, strut, sneer, look at me.

The soldier finishes checking IDs. There are more buses behind us to be checked. The big honcho looks at all of us, sneers one more time and says, 'OK, get back into the bus.'

They didn't ask us anything. I must say that there are times when Latin machismo is the best thing I know. If the guy hadn't been so concerned with showing off to a foreigner he might have wondered who we were, coming from Chalatenango, and asked for IDs. But he didn't.

We arrived in San Salvador, thanked the *compa*, hopped into a cab and went to Metro Centro. What a change. One year in the mountains and then boom into a shopping center à la *gringa*. Too much contrast. After that ordeal we went to the hotel. On the way we stopped at the bus station to check on the schedules. Luis' bus leaves every hour, mine only once a day, in the evening. I couldn't leave that evening because I had to get a visa from the Guatemalan consulate.

We checked into the hotel and Luis was very nervous. We filled out the cards and after a moment Luis asked for another one and took the one he had written on and tore it into tiny pieces and stuck them in his pocket. Inside the room I asked him what happened down there.

'I signed my name backwards!' He was so nervous that he signed his name backwards. His signature is sort of two squiggly lines with a hump at the beginning of each one, he put the hump at the end.

I called up the Guatemalan consulate and they told me that they were closed for vacation and would only open on 3 January. I freaked out because my allotted time in El Salvador would expire in two days, and if I overstayed I would have to present myself to the military. But, he said, there was a consulate in Santa Ana that might be open tomorrow. I called and they said they would be open. I sat on the bed and decided that I'd go to Santa Ana, get a visa, come back – since Susana had told me that I couldn't leave through Santa Ana – stay another night in this damn country and leave the following day.

Luis said I should go through Santa Ana, it was almost on the border. I decided to make that decision when I got there. We agreed to meet at the little *pensión* Tilo told us to stay in in Guatemala City and Luis went off early in the morning. Several hours later I caught a bus to Santa Ana.

I arrived at the little Guatemalan consulate taking up a room in a bank. 'Ah, yes, you called about a visa. No problem, just give me your passport.' I pulled it out, he looked at it and said, 'Oh, that passport. I thought you were an American. That's more of a problem.' Problem, problem, what could the problem be? 'That will cost $20.00.' Oh, OK, no problem. He took my passport and invited me to wait in the back. Several minutes later a little fat man came out of a room and gave me my passport with a visa in it.

And they didn't ask for a signature! Far out! I decided that I was going to get out of El Salvador and that I'd do it through there. I checked around and decided I could take a little common bus to the border and from the border another one to Guatemala City.

We reached the border in half an hour. I walked as nonchalantly as possible to the immigration office. (I had checked my fake entrance stamp with a real one in Lisa's passport – they were almost identical, just a slight matter of spacing.) I walked in, a young lady smiled and reached for my passport. When I gave it to her her smile faded. She was sure I was going to hand her a US passport. She called the head honcho over – the only male in the place – and said, 'such-and-such a passport.' He took it, went over to a desk and turned his back. I lit a cigarette and pretended to be who I was supposed to be. He made a show of going through all the pages – it was new so what was there to check, but do what you want – then a big slap as he stamped it and he turned around and handed it to me. I smiled and walked out into the sun. A soldier went through my bag and off I walked to Guatemala.

In Guatemala I handed in my passport. I was getting used to those 'but I thought you were' looks. I got another stamp and got on a bus.

At the *pensión* I called the Costa Rican consulate. They were closed until 3 January. Hell, I'm going to spend my birthday and New Year's all by myself and with a fake passport. Luis is leaving tomorrow and said he would leave my equipment with the *compa* Susana mentioned in San José.

It feels like weeks have gone by but it was only yesterday morning that I left Chalatenango. Only yesterday, and I've travelled from one world into another. It still hasn't hit me. I am still worried about getting through what I have to get through on this passport.

There is a small library here filled with thrillers and mysteries, just the thing to pass the time. Between books I worry about the Costa Ricans and work on my signature. Every morning and every afternoon I do about 50 of them. Then I burn the paper and flush it down the toilet.

I've booked a flight to San José on the 3rd, late afternoon. By the end of this week I should be free. I hope, I hope. And then? God knows. Firecrackers go off incessantly here. In the streets the vendors yell out, 'Here, get your machine-gun bang-bangs here!' What contrasts.

I must calm myself for tomorrow when I go to the Costa Rican consulate. At least they are not the enemy but if they find me out what will happen? Will they turn me over to the Guatemalan police? When I feel this way I sit and do my signature over and over again and it comes out beautifully, but I figure it won't tomorrow. The worst is over by a long shot – but it's not over until it's over, damn it!

I went to the consulate and they told me that it takes 24 hours to get a visa. Damn! Now in my room, I pace back and forth rehearsing the speech I will give when they inform me tomorrow that I have been denied a visa because my passport is false.

I returned to the consulate with heart thumping. They smiled and handed me my passport with a visa in it! Ha! So now all I have to worry about is getting through the airport here, which is a lot more sophisticated than the border I crossed, then San José airport, and then I'll be all right.

No one batted an eye in either place! This is definitely a good passport. The only thing the Costa Rican immigration officer said was, 'Why so serious in this photograph? Relax!' Yes, sir, I intend to.

Well, I'm almost out. The year is over. I feel that I've failed, no photographs, no notebooks. I must accept the fact that I'll never see them again. At least I have my equipment. If I had my work how much would it change things? I don't know. I'm too much in a daze, too numb, to know or decide anything.

After a couple of hours of being indoors I feel a need to go out. I miss the openness all around. I've lived a year outside and it's strange to be inside and strange to be alone. Living in that front was a collective and outdoor existence. Nature everywhere and you depended on it to hide you, clean you, feed you, quench your thirst.

Manuel, a *compa*, came by and gave me my equipment. I said that I planned to go to the US embassy and see what we could work out. He said that he didn't think that was such a good idea.

'What do you recommend that I do then?'

'Use the one you've been using and go to Mexico. In Mexico you get rid of this one and you'll be alright.'

'I have to go to Mexico with this passport? Do you think it will pass the Mexican authorities?'

'Yes.'

OK. Off to get another visa, off to write the goddamn signature again, off to be nervous until it's all over.

What a trip! I will never make a good spy! (Although I suppose that when the CIA makes you a passport you have all the right connections should anything go wrong.) I flew out of San José, no problem. Then there was a stopover in El Salvador. Ridiculous, I was back in El Salvador!

I arrived at Mexico City airport. The place was jammed. In line I noticed that I had forgotten to sign the back of a paper. Hell, I knelt down on the floor and signed it. It was the worst signature I had ever done. I finally got to the emigration officer. He grabbed my passport and slapped it on the counter. He looked at it, looked at me and asked for another ID.

'Another ID?'

'Yes, I want another ID. Give me your driver's license. Surely you drive.'

'Yes, I do, but not on vacation and I'm on vacation and I don't have it.'

'What are you doing here?'

'I came to visit Mexico.'

'Where are you going to stay?'

I named the hotel.

'Why don't you have your driver's license?'

'Because I'm on vacation.'

Throughout his questioning he was going through my passport inch by inch. At one point he picked it up and looked at the page with my picture up at the light. (I had done the same several times and the punched holes were not exact.)

'What's your profession?'

I told him.

'What's the address of the hotel?'

'I don't know.'

'Are you being met?'

'No.'

'Do you live in Costa Rica?'

'No.'

'Where do you live?'

I told him.

'Are you travelling alone?'

'Yes.'

Then with much drama he slammed the stamp on to the page and signed it with great flourish. I was about to tremble into little pieces. I picked up my camera bag and went off to customs.

At customs the man opened everything.

'What are you doing here?'

I answered.

'First time in Mexico?'

I answered.

He pulled out a plastic bag with shampoo and tampax in it. Pointing to the tampax he asked, 'What's this?'

I explained.

'Are you a student?'

I answered.

He pointed to the shampoo and said, 'OK, tell me what kind of drug that is.'

'Drug? That's shampoo!'

'No, no, no', he said and pointed again to the tampax. 'What kind of drug is it?'

I couldn't believe it. So, this time, in my best Spanish, I told him, in detail, what a tampax was.

'OK. What's in here?'

'One bottle of rum and one of scotch.'

He took out the bottle of scotch, shook it, turned it upside down and smelled the top. I thought, oh, man, we've both read the same newspaper article, cute, very cute.

'What's in here?'

'Cameras.'

'Why so many?'

I answered and he let me go.

May/June 1985

In May the rains begin, again, in El Salvador. I had not heard from anyone down there, neither had any attempt been made, that I knew of, to send my work up to me – I know, they have a war to fight, I understand. So I decided to make one first and last attempt to salvage my work because, if it still existed, it would never make it through another rainy season. I would give myself a month in San José to organize a plan, then into El Salvador and back to the US.

In San José I called the only *compa* I knew and had a phone number for. I didn't know if he was still around or at the same number but there were many things I didn't know about this trip. He was there and we met. I asked him to send a radio message to Esteban saying that I was here and I was prepared to meet anyone, anywhere, any time in El Salvador, to pick up my stuff. 'Whatever he decides I'll be there.'

The *compa* said it would take about ten days to send the message and receive one back.

'That's what I figured. Call me when you hear.'

Approximately ten days later he called and we met. He'd done as I had asked and had received a message from Esteban saying that it was not for him to arrange as my stuff was left in La Dos.

'Shit. OK, send the same message to Susana.'

'That will take another ten days.'

'I know.'

After hanging out in San José for over 20 days waiting to do things their way, it became apparent to me that I could be hanging out in San José for six months and still be waiting. So I came up with my own plan.

I tried to get in touch with the *compa* to tell him my plan but he would not return my calls. Finally I got him and he said he had not gotten back to me because the *compas* had been on a *guinda* and consequently did not respond to his message.

'I have another plan. Let's meet.'

I told him that I was going to go to El Salvador, that I would get my press card from COPREFA (press office of the armed forces giving the only press card that allows you to run around the country), and that I was going to go back to the base I had left from and await my stuff to be sent down the mountain. All I wanted was for him to inform Susana of my plan. 'I'm not interested in an answer. I'm leaving tomorrow. Just tell her that I'm coming. OK?'

I arrived in San Salvador, called a few very close friends, and went to the military headquarters for my press card. At COPREFA I was given a speech about how certain journalists, especially freelancers – referring to me – think 'it's cool to go spend time with the guerrillas, but it's not cool, it's forbidden, and if the press doesn't play by the rules they get thrown out.' Yes, sir. I wouldn't think of spending time with the guerrillas.

After I got my card I met with my friends, told them my plan and asked if anybody could help. One of them knew someone who had contact with the people in the mountains so I went and talked to him. After he decided that I was OK he told me to go talk to a nun that had direct contact with them. Fine.

I went to meet her in some convent, and who did it turn out to be but the nun that came for Christmas! Of course she remembered me.

'I want to send a message to Jessica.'

'Sure.'

I wrote it out and said, 'I'm not interested in a response. I'm going there three days from now. I just want her to be expecting me.'

A group of religious folk, including the nun, were going to a little town next to Jessica's base for a meeting and I got a ride with them. I had arranged for a friend to pick me up two days later at 08:00 hrs at the same crossroads I had left from last December. We got stopped on the way but the clergy were legit and I had my press pass.

Outside the meeting place was a woman waiting for some things the nun had brought. I went to talk to her and she remembered me from Christmas. Great.

'Will you take me to Jessica?'

'Of course.'

We walked about 45 minutes. We got to a house and the woman told someone to go tell Jessica that I wanted to speak to her. Two hours later she returned with a message that Jessica was radioing to Susana about me and would be down in the evening. Good.

Evening came and Jessica and her two assistants arrived. Hello, hello! Jessica said that no message had been sent back to her.

'It doesn't matter. Is the *guinda* over?'

'Yes.'

'Everybody back?'

'Yes.'

'OK, José and I, at dawn tomorrow, are going up those mountains and I'm getting my stuff. We'll be back by evening. OK?'

'But with the *guinda* I don't know where the new headquarters is,' said José.

'It doesn't matter, we'll find out on the way.'

At dawn José and I walked up into those unforgettable mountains. We walked for over four hours. At different places I met *compas* I knew. Some were surprised to see me – 'What, you have come back?'

'No, no, just a short visit.'

Others hadn't known that I had left.

Turning the bend I saw a *compa* who had been Cienfuegos' bodyguard. Hello, hello!

'Do you know where the new headquarters is?'

'Sure, just down there and to the right, you'll see a new camp.'

Walking through the trees I saw a clearing, and sitting in that clearing were Susana, Tilo, Chevo and someone I didn't know. I approached quietly and suddenly stood in front of them.

'Good day *compañeros*!'

Everyone was taken completely by surprise. Susana jumped up saying, 'Good God, look who's here! Taina!' Yes, 'tis I indeed and I've come for my stuff. Susana said that they had to finish the meeting and then we would talk. OK.

As it turned out, there was only one *compa* who knew where my things were buried, and he happened to be both alive and there. He said it would take about four hours. No problem. How about some beans and tortillas. Sure, let's go to the kitchen!

Life was pretty much the same as I had left it. I got to hear the latest *guinda* stories. One last *guinda* story for old time's sake: there was a column of about 250 *compas* consisting of the top honchos of four of the organizations, the radio people, the Comité Zonal, the political/ideological *mara*, *Propa*, etc., moving through the mountains. Most wore uniforms of one sort or another and most had M-16s, but they were not combatants. At dawn, a company of the Atlacatl that had taken one of the highest tops, saw them and radioed headquarters: 'We've just sighted a column of guerrillas. What do we do?'

'How many are there?'

'Many. The columm goes from one mountain to another!'

'Too many. Don't do anything.'

I really do believe in the luck of the guerrilla.

The *compa* finally returned carrying a large mud-covered plastic bag. I looked inside and – lo and behold – it was full of film and notebooks. The sweetest sight I'd seen in a long time. I grinned, picked up the bag, and said, 'It's been great seeing you people. I wish you all the best. *Adiós compas.*'

'What, you're not spending the night?'

Susana came up and told me that they were giving a press conference and handing over prisoners to the Red Cross tomorrow in La Laguna. Didn't I want to stay and go with them tomorrow and photograph it?

'Thanks, Susana, but no thanks, I just want my film and I think the best thing for me to do is get out of here as soon as possible.'

On the way back it poured like hell, but I didn't care – what's a little walk in the rain when you have your long lost work in your arms? Back at Jessica's she told me that an hour after I had left she got a radio message saying that I was not to go up because they didn't know where my stuff was buried. I was to go back to San Salvador and wait. Someone would get it to me. (Must have been that *compa* in the meeting that didn't know me.) Right! But it doesn't matter now because I've got it.

The following morning Jessica asked a woman to accompany me to the crossroads where I was to meet my friend. Then 08:00 hrs came and went. No friend. He is a punctual man. I decided that Ochoa had closed the road to Chalate because he didn't want any press to cover the handing over of the prisoners. The woman with me thought that if the roads were closed we should go back to Jessica's and try again tomorrow.

Very vivid visions of waiting went through my mind and I said, 'Oh, no. I'm getting out of here one way or another. Would you please go over to one of those houses and find out what the bus situation is?'

I was right. The road had been closed by the military and no buses had come through in either direction yet today. But according to normal schedules the next bus should come at 13:00 hrs.

'OK, I'll take it if it comes.'

The bus came right on time and I hopped on. We passed a number of checkpoints and I saw soldiers sprawled out on the ground taking a siesta. Seemed like the show was over.

I arrived at my friend's place.

'I was hoping you wouldn't try to get out today', he said. 'I left at dawn but the military didn't let anybody through. I was going to pick you up tomorrow. But, knowing you, I'm not surprised that you're here!'

He then told me that the nun had called him to say that she was very upset because she had received a note saying that I was not to go to Chalate, that a *compa* would bring my stuff to the capital in a week or so, and I was to wait. Very funny. Had I done it their way who knows how long I would have had to sit in San Salvador waiting for my film. Who knows, and who knows if it would have ever been delivered? Questions I didn't care to think about because I knew the answers. I know, they have a war to fight, I understand, I do, I really do.

The following morning I got out on the first plane going to Miami. Flying over the Guazapa volcano for the nth time I thought, OK, Taina/Wendy, this time, this time you're free!

Notes

1. Agustín Farabundo Martí was exiled from El Salvador in the early 1920s. He went to Guatemala, spent some time in the US and then went and fought with Augusto Sandino against the US Marines in the mountains of Nicaragua. In 1930 he returned to El Salvador and founded the Socorro Rojo Internacional, which worked closely with the Salvadoran Communist party. From 1930 to 1932 he worked with and organized peasant Indians in the western part of the country who were extremely angry with the conversion of their communal lands into private coffee growing estates. Farabundo Martí was arrested for the last time in January 1932 and killed by firing squad. Three days after his arrest the peasant Indians rebelled. The military responded by killing 30,000 peasants in a matter of weeks. This massacre is known in the history of El Salvador as La Matanza (The Killing). One organizer who survived said: 'I believe that the drama of 1932 is for El Salvador what the Nazi barbarity was for Europe ... a phenomenon that completely changed, in the negative sense, the face of a nation ... Since that evil year all of us are other people and I believe that since then El Salvador is another country. Above all else, El Salvador is today the work of that barbarity.'
2. Term used to designate those fighting against the Salvadoran government forces. The guerrilla struggle began in the early 1970s.
3. El Salvador is the smallest country in Central America, the most densely populated in Latin America and one of the poorest in the hemisphere. Sixty per cent of the Salvadoran people are peasant farmers yet 60 per cent of the land is in the hands of 2 per cent of the people. Although El Salvador has been under military rule of one kind or another since the middle of the nineteenth century, it is known for having been under a continuous military dictatorship for 50 years, starting in 1932 – the longest, to date, in Latin America.
4. A controlled zone is territory controlled by the FMLN. To control a zone means to eliminate all Salvadoran government military posts and barracks in an area. The size of the territories has grown as the FMLN has grown in numbers and power. In 1984 one-third of the country was considered to be under FMLN control.
5. US military and economic aid was, at the time of going to press (Dec. 1989), US $1.5 million per day.
6. Frente Farabundo Martí de Liberación Nacional (Farabundo Martí National Liberation Front) was created in 1980 by the ERP, FPL, RN, PRTC and FAL – guerrilla groups that had been active in the country during the 1970s but had operated separately and had their own territories in the countryside.
7. The preferred vehicle of the deathsquads and other paramilitary groups.

8. Fuerzas Populares de Liberación (Popular Forces of Liberation) – one of the five groups in the FMLN. The FPL, formed in 1970, is the oldest guerrilla group. In 1984 it was considered to be, along with the ERP, the largest and strongest of the five groups. On account of the work it has developed with the civilians in its controlled zones I chose it as the group to document. My year in El Salvador was organized and spent with this group.

9. In 1984 there were two guerrilla radio stations operating, clandestinely, in El Salvador: the FPL's Radio Farabundo in Chalatenango, and the ERP's Radio Venceremos in Morazán.

10. A specialized security force originally created in 1912 by the government for the exclusive purpose of maintaining order and enforcing the landlords' law in rural areas. It is known, along with the National Police, for its extreme brutality.

11. The 1982 and 1984 elections in El Salvador were sponsored by the US government so as to give the impression that democracy was 'taking hold' and thus convince the US Congress that it should continue to approve military and economic aid to the country. In a country fighting a civil war it is difficult to imagine that 'free' elections could be held. In 1984 there was an officially declared 'state of siege': there was no freedom of the press, no freedom of assembly, and no opposing political parties were allowed to participate.

12. National Coordination of the Popular Church (CONIP) formed in 1980 after Archbishop Romero's assassination. Most CONIP parishes are located in controlled zones.

13. Christian Democrat José Napoleón Duarte was elected president of El Salvador in 1984. After Guillermo Ungo and Rubén Zamora resigned from the five-man junta created by the October 1979 coup, Duarte was finally allowed to be president, although more for show than anything else. In the 1982 elections he and D'Aubuisson were running for president, but the military informed them that neither would be allowed to be president. In the 1984 elections it was decided, mainly by the Reagan administration, that Duarte would be president as he would create a favorable impression on Congress. This would then free the way for more US military and economic aid to El Salvador.

14. Fuerzas Armadas de Liberación (Armed Forces of Liberation), one of the five groups of the FMLN.

15. Frente Democrático Revolucionario (Democratic Revolutionary Front) was formed in 1980 by a broad coalition of the Social Democratic Party, Christian Democrats who opposed the 3rd junta, trade unions, Church people, professionals, students and small-business people. The FDR is the political arm of the FMLN. In November of that same year six leaders of the FDR were brutally tortured and executed.

16. Ejército Revolucionario del Pueblo (The People's Revolutionary Army), one of the five groups of the FMLN. Their major controlled zone is in Morazán.

17. Resistencia Nacional (National Resistance), one of the five groups of the FMLN. The RN was created by a dissenting group within the ERP after Roque Dalton (Salvadoran poet) was shot by the ERP on the grounds that he was a spy.

18. ERP's radio in Morazán.

19. Roberto D'Aubuisson is a career officer trained in Panama and the International Police Academy in Washington. He became a major in the National Guard but

was thrown out of the army in the 1979 October coup. D'Aubuisson is considered to be the most notorious torturer and deathsquad leader in El Salvador. There is strong evidence that he planned Archbishop Romero's assassination. During the US-backed 1982 elections he became the president of the National Assembly. He is also the leader of the ultraconservative and paramilitary party ARENA – the Nationalist Republic Alliance.

20. Partido Revolucionario de los Trabajadores Centroamericanos (Central American Revolutionary Workers Party), one of the five groups of the FMLN.

21. Guillermo Manuel Ungo was Duarte's running mate in the 1972 elections that were stolen by the army. Then in the October 1979 coup he was one of three civilian members of the five-man junta. But he resigned when he realized that the junta was controlled by the armed forces. He is presently the president of the FDR. Rubén Ignacio Zamora was named minister of the presidency in the October coup, but he also resigned. After his brother was assassinated by unknown masked men he went into exile for the third time. He is presently the FDR's foreign relations person.

22. The Salvadoran Army's best combat commander.